1997

More Fantastic
FUNDRAISERS
for SPORT and RECREATION

William F. Stier, Jr., EdD
State University of New York, Brockport

Human Kinetics

Library of Congress Cataloging-in-Publication Data

Stier, William F.
    More fantastic fundraisers for sport and recreation / William F.
Stier, Jr.
        p.   cm.
    ISBN 0-88011-525-4
    1. Sports--United States--Finance--Handbooks, manuals, etc.
    2. Recreation--United States--Finance--Handbooks, manuals, etc.
    3. Fund raising--United States--Handbooks, manuals, etc.
    4. Nonprofit organizations--United States--Finance--Handbooks,
manuals, etc.   I. Title.
    GV716.S735   1997
    338.4'796--dc21   96-48717
                                                              CIP

ISBN: 0-88011-525-4

Photo on page 102 courtesy of Eddie Feigner; photos on pages 155, 157, and 187 courtesy of Jim Dusen.

Acquisitions Editors: Rick Frey and Scott Wikgren; **Developmental Editor:** Julia Anderson; **Assistant Editor:** Jacqueline Eaton Blakley; **Editorial Assistant:** Coree Schutter; **Copyeditor:** Dena Popara; **Proofreader:** Sarah Wiseman; **Graphic Designer:** Stuart Cartwright; **Graphic Artist:** Francine Hamerski; **Cover Designer:** Jack Davis; **Illustrator:** Tim Stiles; **Printer:** Versa Press

Printed in the United States of America   10 9 8 7 6 5 4 3 2 1

Human Kinetics

Web site: http://www.humankinetics.com/

United States: Human Kinetics, P.O. Box 5076, Champaign, IL 61825-5076
1-800-747-4457
e-mail: humank@hkusa.com

Canada: Human Kinetics, Box 24040, Windsor, ON N8Y 4Y9
1-800-465-7301 (in Canada only)
e-mail: humank@hkcanada.com

Europe: Human Kinetics, P.O. Box IW14, Leeds LS16 6TR, United Kingdom
(44) 1132 781708
e-mail: humank@hkeurope.com

Australia: Human Kinetics, 57A Price Avenue, Lower Mitcham, South Australia 5062
(08) 277 1555
e-mail: humank@hkaustralia.com

New Zealand: Human Kinetics, P.O. Box 105-231, Auckland 1
(09) 523 3462
e-mail: humank@hknewz.com

To my wife, Veronica, and our five children—Mark, Missy, Michael, Patrick, and Will III—for their loving encouragement and continued unselfish support. A special thanks also to Samantha, Katie Lee, Joshua, Michael, Jessica Bree, and Jack.

CONTENTS

PREFACE

This publication is a sequel to the book, *Fundraising for Sport and Recreation,* originally published in 1994. Like its predecessor, this book is practical and user-friendly in its approach to solving the ever-present problem of generating resources for sport, recreation, and other nonprofit organizations.

Following the publication of the earlier book, I repeatedly have been asked by readers to provide additional ideas that can be used to generate money, as well as enthusiasm and positive public relations, for a wide range of nonprofit programs. This sequel, *More Fantastic Fundraisers for Sport and Recreation*, is the result. I have expanded upon the initial publication by providing an additional 70 fundraising projects involving a variety of different techniques and tactics.

Specifically written for sport, recreation, and other nonprofit practitioners seeking fundraising ideas for their respective organizations, this book provides specific, helpful plans for conducting fundraising activities. In these pages are practical ideas for successfully planning and implementing a number of successful fundraising projects that can both generate money and enhance the image of your program.

The ideas provided within this book, like those within its predecessor, are based on proven fundraising concepts. The fundamental fundraising guidelines given throughout the publication should be of practical help to people facing the formidable task of generating additional money and support for their organizations.

As the 21st century approaches, there will be an increasing need for outside fundraising, especially for nonprofit organizations faced with insufficient operating budgets. As a result, organizations involved in sport, recreation, and leisure will continue to need people who are knowledgeable in the art of fundraising and who are capable of meeting the challenges of generating additional financial support. This is especially important given increasing financial needs coupled with limited sources of traditional funding.

Never has there been greater need for individuals who are skilled in fundraising. These people include administrators and recreation leaders; development staff for nonprofit social organizations; coaches, athletic administrators, and booster club members for youth and junior or senior high sports; and coaches and athletic administrators at junior colleges, and 4-year colleges and universities. As I wrote this book, in fact, I received helpful ideas, suggestions, and critiques from people representing these and other organizations.

The fundraising plans outlined in this book include projects that have been used successfully by a variety of recreation and sport organizations—both large and small—to generate additional financial and public support for their programs. My purpose in writing this book is to provide you, the beginner as well as the experienced fundraiser, with the means to assess, organize, and implement successful fundraising projects. Some of these fundraising projects you may be able to implement in your own communities with few, if any, significant changes. Other fundraising projects might require either moderate or substantial alterations to use successfully for your particular situation.

This book is divided into several sections. The first explains how to use the book and presents insight into basic fundraising theories and principles. This section also gives specific suggestions and guidelines for conducting successful fundraising events. The second section provides the Fundraiser Finder, an index for the 70 fundraising projects included within this book. The Fundraiser Finder categorizes each of the projects based on the expected net profit, complexity of the event, number of helpers needed, and amount of money required to initiate the event. The remaining four sections of the book are devoted to the fundraising projects themselves, which are categorized based on their potential net profit.

Each fundraising project includes all of the information you will need to plan and implement the event. This information includes a description of the project; the potential income and other benefits relative to the effort expended; the degree of complexity of the activity; suggestions for when to plan and hold the event; the time requirements to plan and implement the project; the resources needed in terms of facilities, seed money, equipment, and supplies; suggested publicity and related promotional activities; personnel requirements; information about permits or licenses; tips for managing potential financial and legal risks; and specific hints for the success of the project.

The information concerning specific projects, as well as the general fundraising principles cited in the section "How to Use This Book," will enable you to accomplish two objectives. First, you will develop a basic understanding of the components necessary for making any fundraising project a success. Second, you will learn how to apply this basic knowledge, together with your own ideas and an understanding of your unique needs and resources, to plan and implement fundraising activities. It is the combination of fundraising theory and practical advice that makes this book, as well as its predecessor, uniquely valuable to organizers of fundraising events in the world of sport and recreation. Good luck.

HOW TO USE THIS BOOK

Sport and recreation have never been more popular in this country than today. However, this increase in participation has come with an increase in cost. Recreation leaders, coaches, and sport administrators are painfully aware of the financial crunch facing almost all organizations that provide sport and recreation programs, whether such activities are provided within an educational setting, a youth sport organization, a recreation department, or some other nonprofit entity.

The financial needs of sport and recreation programs must be met. Without adequate funding, sport and recreation programs, whatever their intrinsic value, are likely to fail. Thus, securing financial support has become a prime responsibility and challenge facing recreation leaders, sport administrators, and athletic coaches.

In fact, the ability to secure adequate funding is an essential and indispensable skill in the operation of any sport or recreation program. The sport leader who is a competent fundraiser is a valuable asset to any organization. Fundraising has become a fact of life for those involved in sport, recreation, and leisure programs.

A successful fundraising event satisfies four major objectives. First, the event is financially successful; it makes money that you can use to support your organization's many worthwhile activities. Second, the event generates enthusiasm for the fundraising project itself. Third, the event fosters and reinforces a positive image of the organization and its supporters through the exposure, publicity, and public relations associated with the activity. Fourth, the event generates genuine support for the overall efforts and goals of the sponsoring organization.

Although obtaining money is the main objective of most fundraising activities, organizers should recognize that contributed goods and services can be as valuable as cash. Some donated goods (such as paintings, tickets) and services (such as professional car washes, pet grooming) can be auctioned to generate money. Other donated goods (for example, computers, software) and services (for example, legal and accounting advice) can be used in day-to-day operations of the organization or in future fundraising activities. Therefore, organizers should think not only in terms of cash but also of services and goods that may enhance the overall operation of the sponsoring group.

Those in charge of fundraising will find that their individual situations are usually different—sometimes radically so—from the situations in which others must operate. Sometimes specific resources (such as facilities, personnel, equipment, and money) are not available or are inadequate for a particular project. Frequently there are limitations (such as those related to finances, public relations, competition, and location) that will restrict your activities.

Thus, you must look at each fundraising project with a critical eye to see whether the suggestions can simplify or improve some aspect of the fundraising process, if not the total project itself. You must determine what will work in your own community in light of its resources and limitations.

I suggest that you read through all the fundraising projects included in this book to develop an awareness of the similarities and differences among the various methods of fundraising. Many projects contain information and suggestions that are applicable to other fundraising efforts.

You should examine carefully all the projects that use similar fundraising concepts. For example, if you are thinking of having an auction at the local level, you will find it helpful to read all the fundraising projects in this book that use the auction method. Similarly, there are several fundraising efforts that use the sales concept and several that involve food or a concession operation. Reading all the projects based on the same concept will enhance your understanding and competency in creating, developing, and implementing a successful fundraising program.

HOW THIS BOOK IS ORGANIZED

Following this introduction is a Fundraiser Finder, which will help you quickly decide which project will be suitable for your organization. In the Fundraiser Finder each event is listed alphabetically and is assigned an identifying number. To the right of each fundraiser are listed the potential dollar profit (net income), the complexity rating of the event, the number of people needed for planning and implementing the project, the amount of money needed to finance the fundraiser, and the page number in the book where the event is described in detail.

The various fundraising projects are presented in identical formats for ease of comparison and understanding. Details about the following factors are given for each project.

Potential Net Income

An estimated net profit is provided for each fundraising project. Of course, profit will vary from event to event and from community to community, so the figures I provide are only estimates.

Complexity/Degree of Difficulty

Complexity is indicated by the words *low, moderate,* and *high.* These terms indicate the amount of work and time generally involved in planning and implementing the project. The complexity of any event depends on the sponsoring organization's resources, priorities, restrictions, and community climate. What might be difficult for one group might not be as difficult for another.

Description

This section explains the project and addresses details that are necessary for the project's success.

Scheduling

This information includes techniques and strategies for successful event scheduling.

Resources

This general category is broken down into the following subcategories, which provide insight into the resources you will need.

Facilities. This section describes what facilities, if any, are needed for the fundraising event. Where applicable, suggestions are made regarding the specific location of the facilities.

Equipment and Supplies. The necessary equipment and supplies for each event are listed, and suggestions are included on how best to obtain and use such items.

The tools of the trade for the modern fundraiser include not only the telephone but a fax machine, a computer, a printer, and the appropriate software (word processing, database, presentation, graphics, and desktop publishing). Some tools are used to reach potential donors and patrons; other tools are used to create printed materials (programs, signs, and flyers) for the fundraising event itself. The sponsoring organization is not required to purchase such tools. Rather, the volunteers and staff need only to have access to them, preferably for free or at a greatly reduced cost.

Publicity and Promotion. Suggestions regarding the use of publicity and promotional tactics are presented for each fundraising project. The public should be aware that the fundraising project is being sponsored by a worthy, nonprofit organization. Don't hesitate to publicize how the profits will be used within the community.

Time. This category gives the time requirements for the planning and implementation stages, as well as for the actual event.

Expenditures. This section estimates how much money you might have to spend, and for what, in order to conduct the fundraiser. In many cases, it costs money to make money. For example, when projects involve sales, organizers frequently need to purchase (at reduced cost) the items that are to be sold. There is no formula or fixed percentage that you can use as a benchmark for determining how much money should be spent to raise a specific dollar amount. The money spent and profit earned will depend upon your specific situation.

Generally speaking, you should avoid spending money whenever possible. Rather, you should attempt to obtain tools, assets, and resources for free or at reduced cost. If you need poster boards, ask for donations. If signs need to be painted, find someone who will donate the time and expertise. Every dollar not spent is a dollar earned.

Personnel (Staff and Volunteers). Every fundraising effort depends upon personnel, both the paid staff of the sponsoring organization as well as volunteers or boosters. This section provides suggestions regarding the approximate number of people who should be involved with the event and their principal responsibilities and tasks.

In addition to the personnel, there are influential people within any community who can open doors to potential contributors (both individuals and organizations) on behalf of the fundraising group. Identifying and getting help from these influential people are often the keys to conducting a successful fundraising effort.

Risk Management

This category deals with legal risks, such as liability concerns and insurance matters, and with financial risks—both of which could prove disastrous for the fundraising organization if safeguards are not in place. Risk management involves examining worst-case scenarios and then making plans to avoid or minimize any possible negative consequences.

Permits/Licenses

This category explains how to secure any permits, licenses, or permissions you may need in order to carry out the project.

Hints

This category gives suggestions on how to plan, execute, and evaluate the fundraising event. This section also may explain alternative ways to conduct the project. You should consider these hints in light of the individual resources and limitations in your community and within the sponsoring group itself.

GAMBLING AND GAMES OF CHANCE

Special note should be taken of fundraising efforts that involve gambling or games of chance. Many states and communities have laws or ordinances either prohibiting or restricting such activities. Conducting such projects without securing the appropriate permits or licenses, when such are required, can result in serious legal and punitive actions against the sponsoring organization and its leaders. Conscientious fundraisers make sure they meet all legal obligations. Never take a chance by assuming law enforcement agencies may overlook the lack of a permit.

Those fundraising organizers who abide by the philosophy "forgiveness is easier to obtain than permission" should be aware of the potential negative consequences of illegally conducting gambling activities. These consequences can be severe not only in terms of legal penalties but also in negative publicity and tarnished image. The best course of action is to check with your organization's legal counsel before attempting to organize a fundraising project based on gambling or games of chance.

In the state of New York, for example, organizations wishing to conduct such games must secure advance permission both from the New York State Racing and Wagering Board and from the local municipality (through the town clerk) where the event will take place. New York provides two kinds of permits: one for bingo and one for games of chance. The cost of conducting a bingo game is $18.75 per event, whereas games of chance cost $25 per day. Within a specified number of days following the event, a financial statement must be submitted to the state.

ALCOHOLIC BEVERAGES

In order to serve alcoholic beverages at a fundraising event, you must first secure the necessary state and local liquor licenses or permits. The permit requirements vary among locales. Some jurisdictions require one specific permit for hard liquor (scotch, whiskey, vodka, etc.) and another for light spirits (beer, wine, and champagne). Other areas require a specific license if alcohol will be served with food and not purchased separately. Still other types of permits may be issued when a cash bar will be provided or when alcohol will be dispensed on a free basis. You must secure the appropriate permits for your individual community. Of course, the sponsoring organization may have its own restrictions or prohibitions against serving alcohol, so check ahead of time to see what is permitted and what is prohibited.

Organizers of a fundraising event where alcoholic beverages are served also must be alert to the possibility of a patron's becoming intoxicated. The negative consequences are significant not only for the patron but also for the sponsoring organization and the person who served the alcohol. Sponsors and planners of an event where a person consumes an excessive amount of alcohol are increasingly being held responsible for the drinker's actions. No sport or recreation group wants to be involved in a tragedy or scandal involving alcohol. Those responsible for planning the fundraising project must take the following assertive actions to prevent both underage drinking and overindulgence by those of legal age:

- Post signs indicating that patrons will be asked for appropriate identification, and then carefully scrutinize the ID cards.
- Do not serve individuals under legal age or those who already have consumed enough alcohol.
- Make arrangements with a local cab company to drive home patrons who have overindulged in drink, or provide designated drivers from among the volunteers of the sponsoring group.
- Encourage people attending the event to team up with friends who are willing to be designated drivers.

These plans will help prevent the negative consequences of excessive alcohol consumption and driving under the influence. Such precautions also will enhance the public's image of the sponsors as being sensible, caring, and proactive.

SALES

Many fundraising projects involve door-to-door sales. Teaching adult and student volunteers how to sell successfully means teaching how to

- identify and qualify a potential customer,
- approach the prospect,
- explain the product or service,
- emphasize the benefits to the potential purchaser,
- explain the nature of the nonprofit sponsoring organization,
- clarify how the money will benefit young people or sport or recreation programs,
- handle objections,
- thank the prospect whether or not a purchase was made, and
- maintain accurate records.

Overaggressive sales tactics should be strongly discouraged. Remember, the prospective customer should be left with a positive image of both the salesperson and the organization that the salesperson represents.

Whenever young people are expected to sell door-to-door, they first need to receive appropriate safety instruction and sales training. Proper safety instruction teaches children to travel in pairs, be accompanied by an adult or older sibling, sell only within their own neighborhood unless accompanied by an adult, obey all traffic laws, and not venture out after dusk.

The time during which volunteers and staff are involved in the selling process is referred to as the *selling window*. In many instances, the selling window is kept to a minimum, perhaps 3 to 4 weeks. The organizers want a concentrated selling effort within a limited time period rather than a prolonged effort that might result in the loss of enthusiasm and the reduced effectiveness of the sales force.

SALES TAX

Laws vary among states regarding the collection of sales tax for fundraising activities by nonprofit organizations. The question of whether it is necessary to collect sales tax arises when the sponsoring organization sells tickets, merchandise, or concession items. The county tax collector or a representative of the state department of revenue will be able to answer many questions in this regard. You might also consult an attorney or accountant to obtain expert advice about these complicated laws.

PERMITS, LICENSES, AND PERMISSIONS

Some fundraising activities involve door-to-door sales of tangible or intangible items—the most common being tickets, candy, chances, and the like. More and more communities are passing ordinances that prohibit, restrict, or regulate door-to-door sales.

Some communities have ordinances that restrict the activities of *transient retail* merchants. A transient retail business is frequently defined as a business conducted for less than 6 months. It can be located in the street; on the sidewalk; in front of a building; or within a building, motor vehicle, or tent. The transient retail merchant ordinance usually is aimed at restricting or regulating flower vendors, furniture salespersons, car washers, and art merchants who display their merchandise and services at street intersections or in parking lots.

Licensing fee exemptions commonly exist for charitable organizations, groups from area school districts or colleges, recreation departments, city-sponsored organizations, and nationally recognized service organizations or clubs. However, not all communities provide such blanket exemptions. Therefore you should check with the local municipal office that issues permits or licenses (most likely the town clerk or bureau of licenses) to see what the requirements are before initiating a fundraising effort that might fall under the local hawking, peddling, and soliciting ordinance.

When concession or food operations are involved in a fundraising project, you must follow all health department regulations for food storage, preparation, and sales, and you must secure all appropriate permits and licenses that regulate food and concession operations. Such permits usually may be secured from the municipal offices or from the office of the town clerk.

Securing permission and various permits and licenses is only half the battle. The other half is adequately informing the paid staff and volunteers about what the permits, licenses, and permissions require and allow. For example, the licenses and permits that regulate alcohol sales have many restrictions that must be strictly adhered to. Organizers of an event are responsible for seeing that the staff members and volunteers fully understand and abide by the constraints of the licenses.

INSURANCE AND LIABILITY

Organizers of fundraising efforts should always be aware of the potential for injuries and accidents, which can result in lawsuits. The need for insurance to provide liability protection for those involved with the fundraising activity should be thoroughly investigated during the planning stages of the event. Adequate insurance coverage must be available to protect the owner(s) of the site where the fundraising activity will take place, the sponsoring organization, and those individuals who are involved with the project, either as volunteers or as paid staff. This coverage often is included in a blanket insurance policy that covers both the particular facility and the activities that take place within the facility.

RECORD KEEPING

Successful fundraising is not possible without accurate and timely record keeping. Everyone involved (the organizers, the volunteers, and even the support groups) must keep some kind of records. Some items of documentation that often are kept include the following:

- Records of prospects
- Past donors
- Customers
- Alumni
- Inventory
- Vendors
- Budgets
- Income
- Expenses
- Pledges
- Items purchased for later sale
- Insurance
- Taxes
- Permits and licenses
- Minutes or summaries of meetings
- Copies of letters received and sent
- Evaluations of past fundraising projects

One area of concern to all fundraisers is money. Where money is concerned, two key words are *accountability* and *security*. Many schools and recreation departments require that all income from fundraising efforts be deposited in a special activity account. All checks issued on such accounts usually require two (and sometimes three) signatures. Periodic reports of expenses and income (reconciliations and audits) are made to the appropriate parties. Organizers must pay special attention to financial record keeping; nothing can tarnish the reputation of a fundraising organization more effectively than mistakes or scandals associated with the handling of money.

SCHEDULING FUNDRAISING ACTIVITIES

In terms of scheduling, there are three kinds of fundraising activities. First, there is the project that can be conducted only once. For example, scheduling The King and His Court (fundraiser 29) as a softball opponent is probably a one-time event. Second, there are efforts that lend themselves to being held annually. For example, at the Annual Sports Hall of Fame Luncheon (fundraiser 28), notables are inducted every year. Third, some events can be repeated in the future but do not lend themselves to being held every year. Examples are the All-Star Circus (fundraiser 20) and the Community Afghan Sale (fundraiser 47).

There are three significant advantages to implementing a fundraising project that can be repeated, either as an annual event or as a periodic activity. First, people involved in planning and implementing an earlier occurrence of the event will have acquired experience with the project, thus making their subsequent efforts more efficient. Second, members of the public who enjoyed attending or taking part in the fundraising activity in the past are likely to repeat their experience. Third, many people may learn of the fundraising activity through word of mouth and be willing to become involved in the next repeat of the project.

A strategy that many promoters use to maximize profits is to combine fundraising activities. Examples are the Mini Golf Putt-Putt and Raffle (fundraiser 7), and the addition of a concession stand to the Peek-a-Boo Auction (fundraiser 19). Organizers should always be on the lookout for ways to increase profitability and to enhance exposure by staging two or more activities at the same time and site.

THERE IS MORE THAN ONE WAY TO DO ANYTHING

There is no single way to conduct any specific fundraising project. Fifty different organizations could devise 50 different ways to organize and implement one type of event. Thus, it is up to you to decide whether to copy exactly the projects outlined in this book or to adapt the ideas and concepts to suit your particular situation.

Good luck in your search for a suitable fundraising project to fit your needs. After reading this book you will have a sound understanding of each of these projects. Better still, you will possess a better overall concept of the components of the fundraising process itself. Best of all, you will be able to use the ideas and tactics outlined in this book to plan and implement any number of fundraising projects that will net your organization increased enthusiasm for your event, genuine support for your overall efforts and goals, a more positive public image, and additional resources.

FUNDRAISER FINDER

Fundraiser	Number	Net profit	Complexity	Number of people needed	Seed money needed	Page
Affinity Credit Card Sponsorship	44	$6,000	Moderate	6-9	$50	145
All-Star Circus	20	$3,450	Low	37-50	$1,150	76
Alumni Keepsake Publication	10	$2,000	Moderate	22-29	$500	45
Annual Fall Craftfest	67	$20,000	High	53-105	$2,000	212
Annual Fundraising Campaign	53	$7,500	Moderate	16-22	$350	171
Annual Spring Barbecue	63	$14,000	High	33-54	$1,000	201
Annual Sports Hall of Fame Luncheon	28	$3,500	Moderate	16-18	$500	99
Backward Raffle	60	$11,600	Moderate	30-34	$900	192
Beach Towels for Sale	42	$6,000	Low	31-53	$100	139
Bed Race	24	$4,000	Moderate	22-28	$400	88
Bowl-a-Thon	46	$6,000	Moderate	53-57	$50	151
Candy Bar Sale	40	$6,000	Low	52-78	$100	133
Cashola Delight	15	$2,500	Low	41-42	$30	60
Celebrity Auction	27	$4,000	Low	12-18	$550	96

Fundraiser	Number	Net profit	Complexity	Number of people needed	Seed money needed	Page
Celebrity Roast	66	$16,000	High	42-63	$750	209
Coat Check Service	33	$4,400	Low	6-9	$100	113
Community Afghan Sale	47	$6,363	Moderate	6-12	$150	154
Country Calendar and Cookbook Sale	9	$2,000	Low	36-42	$10	43
Daffodil and Tulip Bulb Sale	22	$3,500	Low	45-59	$100	82
Date Auction and Dinner	51	$7,500	Moderate	63-89	$200	165
Discounting Tickets to Corporations and Businesses	57	$11,000	Moderate	8-12	$250	183
Evening Out at Home	70	$29,750	High	30-40	$250	220
Exam Care Packages for Students	11	$2,000	Moderate	37-43	$500	48
Fall Birdseed Sale	8	$1,850	Low	42-46	$150	40
Family-Style Pork Supper	17	$2,500	Moderate	21-27	$200	66
Flag Day Sale	12	$2,400	Low	36-47	$100	51
Gift Wrapping	36	$4,800	Moderate	35-55	$200	121
Halloween Haunted Hayrides	43	$6,000	Moderate	41-54	$400	142

Fundraiser	Number	Net profit	Complexity	Number of people needed	Seed money needed	Page
Home Run Fundraising Program	34	$4,500	Low	40-50	$200	116
Indoor Winter Walkabout	52	$7,500	Moderate	107-160	$150	168
Kids' Day Off	59	$11,500	Moderate	30-45	$100	189
Licensed Merchandise and Apparel Sales	45	$6,000	Moderate	26-42	$750	148
Lift-a-Thon	21	$3,500	Low	26-42	$100	79
Limousine Scavenger Hunt	32	$4,400	Low	27-34	$100	110
Lip Synch Contest	14	$2,350	Low	20-27	$200	57
Magazine Sales	49	$7,000	Moderate	50-75	$100	160
Membership Drive for the Sport Support Group	69	$25,000	Moderate	32-38	$1,000	217
Memorial Gifts	64	$15,000	High	3-6	$250	204
Mini Golf Putt-Putt and Raffle	7	$1,500	Low	6-10	$100	38
Nite at the Races	56	$11,000	Moderate	23-32	$1,400	180
100-Square Sport Pool	6	$1,450	Low	11-17	$50	35
One Million Pennies	54	$9,800	Low	5-10	$200	174

Fundraiser	Number	Net profit	Complexity	Number of people needed	Seed money needed	Page
Parachute Bingo	62	$12,430	High	52-61	$900	198
Peek-a-Boo Auction	19	$3,000	Moderate	47-58	$100	72
Perfect Gift for Secretaries Week	31	$4,500	Moderate	37-54	$500	107
Personalized Athletic Footwear	26	$4,000	Low	21-37	$50	93
Photos With Life-Size Stand-Up Stars	48	$6,750	Low	2-4	$500	157
Pie Toss	25	$4,000	Low	10-17	$50	91
Piggyback Fundraising Solicitation Letter	41	$6,000	Low	5	$200	136
Postseason Sport Banquet	3	$750	Low	7-13	$250	26
Reunion of Championship Athletic Team	5	$1,000	Moderate	18-25	$250	32
Rotational Advertisement Sign	58	$11,400	Low	2-3	$3,600	186
Santa's Workshop	35	$4,000	High	35-50	$500	118
Scoreboard Sponsorship	4	$1,000	Low	4-7	$50	29
Screen-Printed Scarves for Sale	13	$2,450	Moderate	21-27	$50	54
Selling Christmas Trees	39	$5,900	Moderate	30-50	$100	131

Fundraiser	Number	Net profit	Complexity	Number of people needed	Seed money needed	Page
Specialized Sport/ Activity Clinic	1	$600	Low	7-14	$100	20
Sponsorships for Parts of a Facility	61	$11,945	Moderate	6-12	$130	195
Street Fund Drive	50	$7,500	Low	96	$400	163
Tailgate Parties	30	$4,000	Moderate	31-37	$300	104
Team and Individual Sport Photographs	2	$750	Low	1-2	$25	23
Ten a Month Club	68	$21,500	Moderate	14-23	$200	215
The King and His Court Sport Exhibition	29	$4,000	Moderate	31-38	$450	101
Toy Fair	65	$15,800	High	38-52	$1,700	206
Tree of Lights	55	$10,500	Moderate	22-29	$410	178
Trip Packages to a Professional Sport Contest	23	$3,520	Moderate	16-22	$500	85
Turkey Raffle	38	$5,500	Low	27-28	$150	128
Value Rummage Sale	16	$2,500	Moderate	41-50	$50	63
Win-a-Car Basketball Toss	37	$4,900	Moderate	40-55	$750	124
Youth Soccer Tournament	18	$2,500	Moderate	26-32	$400	69

PART I

FUNDRAISERS GENERATING UP TO $3,000

Specialized Sport/ Activity Clinic

POTENTIAL NET INCOME

$600

COMPLEXITY/DEGREE OF DIFFICULTY

Low

DESCRIPTION

The sponsoring organization conducts a clinic where participants are instructed in the skills of a particular sport or activity. Instructors teach a competitive or recreational sport, such as soccer, golf, or swimming, or they teach a hobby activity, such as glass blowing, flower arranging, or painting. The age of participants can range from young children to seniors. The level of instruction can range from beginning to advanced. There may be a single clinic provided or a series of different clinics offered throughout the year. Each clinic can be both a profit maker and a vehicle for positive public relations for the sponsoring organization.

Profit for the sponsoring agency is derived from charging admission to the clinic(s). The price of admission will depend upon the number of hours of instruction involved, the equipment and supplies needed, the number of participants expected at the clinic, and so forth. Charge what the market will bear. Some groups charge $20 per person, above expenses. Therefore if a typical clinic attracts 30 participants and each pays $25, the net profit will be $600.

SCHEDULING

These are day clinics; that is, they are not overnight experiences. The clinics typically are held on week nights or on weekend afternoons during the school year. During the summer months, clinics scheduled for youngsters and school-age children can be held anytime during the week.

RESOURCES

Facilities: A suitable facility for teaching the sport or activity is necessary. Adequate parking space, practice areas, and locker and shower facilities (for sport activities) must be available.

Equipment and Supplies: The organization provides all equipment and supplies needed to participate in the sport or activity being taught. First-aid supplies must be on hand.

Publicity and Promotion: Announcements in the area's news media and in the sponsoring organization's own publication can be very productive. Announcements also can be made at other community events. Signs should be displayed in places of business within the community. Notices for youth clinics can be distributed to area schools.

Time: The clinics themselves can be one-time events or can take place over a number of days or weeks. The organization may hold a single clinic or may sponsor a number of clinics involving different activities or sports. Each clinic session can range from 1 to 4 hours, depending upon the sport or activity, the availability of the facility, and the level of instruction.

Expenditures: Plan to spend $100 to get the clinic projects off the ground, mainly for supplies and for promotional and publicity efforts. The use of the facility should always be free to the sponsoring group, thereby reducing the cost of the clinics for the participants. All teachers should be volunteers or staff. Supplies and equipment are either donated or purchased at reduced cost. All expenses must be factored into the eventual fee charged for participation in the clinics. This includes the cost of T-shirts or hats printed with the name of the clinic and the sponsoring agency, if these are to be given to the participants.

Personnel (Staff and Volunteers): Volunteers (5-10) and staff (2-4) are needed to organize and promote the clinics and to instruct the classes.

RISK MANAGEMENT

There is little financial risk involved because the clinics are not provided unless there are sufficient prepaid registrants. To reduce liability exposure, a volunteer who is certified in both first aid and

CPR should be present. Also, be sure to get the parents' written permission for their youngsters' participation.

PERMITS/LICENSES

Check with the local health department or state department of social services to determine whether there are any regulations governing the conduct of a clinic.

HINTS

To prevent frustrating the participants, be sure to provide sufficient time for them to practice the skills that they have been taught. Instructors should not progress too quickly or proceed at too high a skill level. Remember that each clinic is an opportunity to enjoy oneself while increasing one's knowledge and skill in a physical activity.

Clinics can be organized around different categories of participants. For example, there can be the "father-and-son" or "mother-and-daughter" clinic concept; a clinic for preschool children; or an activity clinic for seniors. The possibilities are endless. The organizers are limited only by their imaginations; by the availability of (free) facilities, equipment, and supplies; and by the interest of potential participants.

Team and Individual Sport Photographs

POTENTIAL NET INCOME

$750

COMPLEXITY/DEGREE OF DIFFICULTY

Low

DESCRIPTION

The sponsoring organization makes arrangements with a professional photographer to take color photographs of the athletes, cheerleaders (if any), coaches, and sport leaders. Team and group pictures are taken, as well as individual snapshots. The photographer provides one free copy of each individual team or group photograph to the sponsoring organization (for possible display in a facility or for inclusion within an scrapbook). The photographer's profit results from the sale of individual and group photos to the coaches, managers, athletes, cheerleaders, and relatives of the athletes. The sport organization receives a percentage (10 percent to 15 percent) of the gross sales.

SCHEDULING

Settle the financial arrangements with the photographer well in advance of the start of the season. The actual photo session can be scheduled during the early part of the season. If the photos are to be taken outdoors, make alternate plans in case of rain. Allow several weeks of advance publicity of this event to make parents aware of the opportunity to purchase photographs of various sizes (each within a cardboard frame) of their children.

RESOURCES

Facilities: Photographs may be taken at the sport site.

Equipment and Supplies: Letters or information sheets are sent to the parents of the youngsters and to other potential purchasers informing them of the opportunity to purchase the photographs. Participants should be in uniform for the photo session.

Publicity and Promotion: This event is publicized both as a fund-raiser for the sponsoring entity and as a service to the parents. The photographs are promoted as ideal gifts for grandparents and other relatives and as wonderful keepsakes for the family album. Parents are notified through letters or information sheets taken home by the youngsters. Information also can be shared at prior team or organization meetings involving parents.

Time: Advance planning and negotiation with the professional photographer can be accomplished in a few days. The time required to take the photographs is minimal, probably 10 to 20 minutes per group. All of the photos may be taken on a single day unless there are several teams having their pictures taken.

Expenditures: Allot up to $25 for promotional expenses, mainly to pay for stationery and stamps. Ideally, these can be obtained on a donated basis from supporters, boosters, or parents.

Personnel (Staff and Volunteers): One sport leader or designated individual can be given the responsibility for working out the details with the photographer. The recognized leader of the sport organization should communicate directly, in writing, with the parents to make them aware of the opportunity to purchase photographs of their youngsters. Coaches should be on hand during the photo session(s) to maintain order among the youngsters.

RISK MANAGEMENT

The sponsoring organization must ensure that representatives of the photography company do not use high-pressure sales tactics with potential purchasers of the photographs. Acceptable marketing methods must be spelled out in advance. Photographers desiring repeat business next season will have a vested interest in satisfying the organizers' wishes in terms of the quality of the photos and how they are marketed. Full disclosure of the financial arrangements between the sport organization and the photography business, including the profit potential accruing to the sport entity, should be shared in advance with the parents. There is no financial risk associated with this fundraiser.

PERMITS/LICENSES

None

HINTS

The promotional emphasis should be that this is both a service to the parents and a fundraiser for the organization. Publicize how the profits will be used in the community. Assure parents that they can buy reasonably priced, high-quality individual and team photos of their children without being subjected to high-pressure sales tactics. This project works equally well with school bands, choirs, and other nonsport groups.

Postseason
Sport Banquet

POTENTIAL NET INCOME
$750

COMPLEXITY/DEGREE OF DIFFICULTY
Low

DESCRIPTION
Following the conclusion of a team's season, the sponsoring organization holds a dinner banquet in which the participants, their parents, and the fans are recognized. The group presents awards in the form of plaques and trophies, and verbally thanks those who volunteered their services during the past season. Skits, old movies, pictures of the team and individual players, and a highlight video of the past season can be a part of the evening's festivities.

Profits are derived from the sale of tickets to the dinner. Meals are served gratis to the athletes, cheerleaders (if any), coaches, the master of ceremonies, and special guests. Everyone else pays for their dinner. The price of tickets is calculated to generate a net profit of $10 per person. Tickets are sold only in advance.

SCHEDULING
The banquet is scheduled for a Friday or Saturday evening following the conclusion of the team's season.

RESOURCES
Facilities: Any site that can accommodate the number of people expected will do. For large teams, the guests can easily top 100 in paid attendance. A school cafeteria might be available, but it may lack the desired atmosphere. Better yet, a restaurant or party house (large restaurant-type facility with banquet and party rooms of various sizes) might be secured for the event.

Equipment and Supplies: Invitations, envelopes, and postage are necessary. Volunteers create flyers, posters, decorations, and the memorabilia to be given to each of the athletes. These items can be obtained on a donated basis or at very little cost. If old movies, photos, and a highlights video or film are to be shown, these items must be obtained, screened, and organized prior to the date of the banquet. The restaurant or caterer is responsible for all food and drink.

Publicity and Promotion: Publicity for the dinner can involve extensive word of mouth coupled with posters displayed within the community's businesses and organizations. The news media should provide announcements of the upcoming banquet as part of their public-service announcements. Putting announcements in the area's advertising periodicals will help remind people of the upcoming event.

Time: Reserve the facility 6 to 8 months in advance. Allow up to 3 weeks to iron out all of the details for the banquet and to obtain the awards to be distributed. Tickets should be on sale for no more than 3 to 4 weeks. Plan to spend 2 to 3 hours on preparations on the day of the banquet. The dinner lasts about 3 hours. Cleanup activities consume 1 to 2 hours.

Expenditures: Individual awards to be given to selected athletes and staff are donated or obtained at reduced cost. For large teams, plan to spend around $250 for awards, publicity expenses, and odds and ends. The cost of the food will vary depending upon the menu and the number of reservations made. Plan to spend between $6 and $12 per person for food (which includes the use of the facility). Once the cost of the meals has been established, organizers can set ticket prices to generate a net profit of $10 per paying attendee.

Personnel (Staff and Volunteers): Volunteers (5-10) and staff (2-3) help to organize the event, prepare and mail invitations, obtain souvenirs and memorabilia, set up decorations, and keep track of reservations and cash received.

RISK MANAGEMENT

The legal exposure associated with this fundraiser is minimal. The fact that all tickets are sold in advance limits the potential financial risks.

PERMITS/LICENSES

If the dinner is to be held at the organization's own site, there may be a need for a special food permit for the dinner. Check with the local health department, board of health, or municipal office.

HINTS

This type of fundraiser can become a highly anticipated annual affair. People look forward to being together following an athletic season to discuss the highlights and to provide recognition to those who made the season possible. Even when the team's record is less than sterling, the end-of-season banquet can be a very successful event. It even can have significant healing and regenerative effects upon the participants. Since many athletic teams and recreational organizations have some type of banquet following a season-long activity, making the dinner into a fundraiser enables the organizers to benefit financially from the event.

Scoreboard Sponsorship

POTENTIAL NET INCOME
$1,000

COMPLEXITY/DEGREE OF DIFFICULTY
Low

DESCRIPTION
For each season of a competitive team, a local business can become a "scoreboard sponsor" by having a professionally created business sign attached to that team's scoreboard. If more than one scoreboard is used, the sponsor can attach a sign to each. The sponsor pays $1,000 per season (plus the cost of creating and installing the sign) for the privilege of having that company's name and advertising slogan associated with the team organized by the sport or recreation organization. In some communities the sponsorship fee may be more or less, depending on what the market will bear.

SCHEDULING
The organization solicits prospective scoreboard sponsors several months prior to the start of the sport season for which the advertising will be sold. The advertising may be renewed for the subsequent season on a preferred basis.

RESOURCES
Facilities: The sport site must have one or more highly visible scoreboards. There also must be a large spectator seating capacity.

Equipment and Supplies: A professionally prepared sign is the only equipment needed.

Publicity and Promotion: The organization promotes scoreboard sponsorship on the basis of two major points. First, the scoreboard advertising is good business because the scoreboard sponsor's sign will be located in a highly visible location at all home games throughout the season of a particular team. Second, the money generated from the scoreboard sponsorship will go to a nonprofit organization to support a worthy cause.

Time: Planning this fundraiser can take 1 to 2 weeks. Allocate 6 weeks to find a sponsor and to have the sign designed, created, and attached to the scoreboard. After the season the signs are removed and either stored for possible future use or disposed of.

Expenditures: This fundraiser costs $50 or less to initiate. The cost of creating an appropriate sign can range from $100 to $250, but the scoreboard sponsor pays this expense. Attempt to obtain the completed sign at a reduced cost or for free because this will encourage businesses to become sponsors. Some businesses will provide a ready-made logo and advertising copy for the sign. Others will have their own sign created (therefore maintaining quality control) according to the dimensions specified by the sport or recreation organization.

Personnel (Staff and Volunteers): A small number of volunteers (3-5) and staff (1-2) can form an effective marketing force in selling this concept to area businesses. Securing a volunteer who is a professional sign maker is a coup indeed.

RISK MANAGEMENT

There are no financial risks involved in this fundraiser because the sponsor pays to create the sign and to attach it to the scoreboard. The liability exposure is minimal if a professional installs the sign. The only real risk associated with this fundraising project is in the content of the advertising on the scoreboard. The content must be appropriate for and inoffensive to everyone. This may limit the types of businesses that the organizing group may approach. For example, tobacco, alcohol, and gambling entities might not be suitable businesses from which to solicit sponsorship.

PERMITS/LICENSES

None

HINTS

There are as many opportunities for securing scoreboard sponsors as there are different teams organized by the sport or recreation organization. There might be 4, 8, 10, or more scoreboard sponsors during a given year if the sport or recreation organization offers that many different competitive teams that meet the criteria of having suitable scoreboards and large spectator followings. This fundraising effort can be advantageous for all types of organizations that are involved in offering sport competition. For example, youth sport groups (Little League, midget football, soccer), high school and collegiate teams, and recreation departments all can find scoreboard sponsors willing to pay in exchange for having their business advertising attached to the scoreboard for all to see.

Sponsors want to get a lot of bang for their buck when it comes to advertising. Those sports that attract the greatest number of spectators will be most attractive to potential business sponsors. Advertisers also like to be associated with winning teams.

Reunion of Championship Athletic Team

POTENTIAL NET INCOME

$1,000

COMPLEXITY/DEGREE OF DIFFICULTY

Moderate

DESCRIPTION

Athletes and coaches associated with a former championship team are brought together by the sponsoring organization for a special dinner. There are two purposes for the event. First, these people are honored for their prior achievements; second, funds are raised for the sponsoring organization through the sale of advance tickets. Each ticket is priced to provide a $10 profit over the cost of the meal and the use of the facility.

SCHEDULING

The special recognition dinner can be scheduled for any evening. However, a Friday or Saturday evening is usually preferable.

RESOURCES

Facilities: A dining facility that comfortably will seat between 100 and 150 patrons plus those sitting at the head table is required. Adequate and safe parking also is necessary. A restaurant or party house that has experience dealing with large groups is recommended, although the sponsoring group's own facility might suffice.

Equipment and Supplies: Volunteers and staff create posters to promote this special event. They also obtain invitations, envelopes, stamps, and decorations. Awards are needed for the honored individuals. Promoters locate old photos, scrap albums, and newspaper articles that detail the exploits of the former athletes and coaches. These items are displayed on tables before and during the banquet. A projector is needed if the sponsors want to present a slide show of old photographs that have been converted to slides for this event. A high-quality microphone and a good sound system should be available within the facility. If the banquet is held at the sponsoring group's own site, the organizers also must obtain all of the equipment and supplies required to put on a formal dinner.

Publicity and Promotion: Invitations are mailed to individuals and organizations. Members, fans, and supporters of the sponsoring organization receive special invitations, as do the family members and friends of those to be honored. Posters can be displayed throughout the area at the sites of various businesses and organizations, some of which may serve as ticket outlets. The news media can publicize the honor banquet prior to the date, then provide follow-up coverage.

Time: This event can be planned within 2 weeks. The sponsors may need to reserve the party house or restaurant 6 to 8 months prior to the event, depending upon how far in advance the facility is booked. The time devoted to promoting and publicizing this event takes 4 to 5 weeks. Cocktails begin at 6:30 P.M., with dinner at 7:15. The dinner lasts about 90 minutes, after which the formal recognition phase of the evening's festivities begins. Allow 2 hours to clean up after the event if the banquet is held at the organization's own site.

Expenditures: Plan to spend $150 on promotional and publicity activities, including sending the invitations. Allocate another $100 for awards (if not donated) to be given to those persons being honored.

Personnel (Staff and Volunteers): A talented, experienced, and competent master of ceremonies is an absolute must if the event is to be a success. Several volunteers (17-23) and a small staff (1-2) are required to organize and implement this fundraiser, especially in the areas of promotion and ticket sales. An additional 10 to 15 helpers are needed to put on the dinner if the sponsoring organization's own facility is used.

RISK MANAGEMENT

Those people to be honored must show up for the event. This is imperative. Nothing could be worse than to plan an honor banquet and then have a significant number of the guests of honor not attend. If alcohol is served, the organizers should take steps to prevent excessive drinking and to prevent driving while under the influence.

Those who might have had too much to drink must be refused more alcohol. The availability of designated drivers or free taxicab rides is a wise move both in terms of reducing liability exposure and in creating positive public relations.

PERMITS/LICENSES

If the banquet is to be held at the sponsoring organization's own site, the organizers may need to obtain food and alcohol permits. Check with the health department or municipal offices, such as the town clerk.

HINTS

The more people who will be honored and who will receive recognition, the greater the number of friends and relatives who will attend as paying patrons. This should be kept in mind when organizing the honors banquet and when planning the list of individuals to receive special invitations.

100-Square Sport Pool

POTENTIAL NET INCOME
$1,450

COMPLEXITY/DEGREE OF DIFFICULTY
Low

DESCRIPTION

A sport pool is planned around an athletic contest that is scored, usually a special event such as the Super Bowl. On a large poster, 100 squares are drawn—10 across and 10 down—that are numbered consecutively from 0 to 9 horizontally across the top and also vertically down the left side, comprising a pool grid. The participants purchase one or more squares at $25 each. The location of each contestant's square is not known until after all of the squares have been purchased. Then the participants or their representative(s)

draw blindly from a box of numbers ranging from 00 to 99. The location of each square on the pool grid is determined according to two numbers: a horizontal number (which is matched with the first digit of each number drawn) and a vertical number (matched with the second digit of each drawn number). For example, the number 35 would match the square that is located third across and fifth down the grid. After the numbers have been drawn, the participants' names are written in the corresponding pool board squares. Of the $2,500 paid by the participants for the squares, $250 is paid to each of four winners. These winners are determined by matching their pool numbers to the combined scores of the two teams at the end of the first quarter, at halftime, at the end of the third quarter, and at the end of the game.

The organizers might want to piggyback the sport pool with a party involving food and drink before, during, and after a big game, during which the cash prizes are awarded. If a party is planned, there is an admission charge to cover the cost of the food, drink, and other expenses, as well as to provide an additional source of net profit.

SCHEDULING

This type of sport pool can be scheduled for any popular sport contest that is scored.

RESOURCES

Facilities: Locate a site where the large poster can be displayed with the names of the contestants written in the individual squares. Two or more identical posters can be displayed at different locations. If the sport pool involves a party where participants are able to watch big-screen televisions, the site must be large enough for the participants to watch the game comfortably.

Equipment and Supplies: Several large poster sheets, felt-tipped pens, tables, a record-and-receipt book, chairs, and flyers are necessary. If a television party is planned to coincide with the game, the sponsoring organization must supply big-screen TVs, additional tables, food, drink, and decorations.

Publicity and Promotion: This type of gambling project is best promoted by word of mouth. Pool grid squares can be sold from tables set up for this purpose at various athletic or recreation events sponsored by the organizing group.

Time: This project can be organized in less than a week. The selling window should not extend beyond 3 to 4 weeks. If a party is to be held, allow 1 to 2 hours to set up for the event and 1 hour to clean up afterward.

Expenditures: Almost everything associated with this project in terms of equipment and supplies should be donated or loaned. A local TV rental business or individuals should loan the television sets. Plan to spend less than $50, mainly for promotional and publicity efforts. When a party is held in connection with the sport pool, the sponsors pay the cost of food and drinks out of the money gained by the admission fees.

Personnel (Staff and Volunteers): Several volunteers (10-15) and a small staff (1-2) are needed to plan and implement this fundraising effort. In addition to obtaining donated and loaned equipment and supplies, they should be actively involved in marketing and selling the squares.

RISK MANAGEMENT

Since the money is collected prior to the start of the contest, there is no financial risk involved. Be sure that everyone understands the rules of the sport pool. It is wise to have all of the rules clearly printed and given to each contestant when the square is purchased. The fun of a sport pool is ruined if disgruntled participants think that the contest was not fair. If alcoholic beverages are available at a party that is held in conjunction with the sport pool, the sponsors must attempt to ensure that no one drinks to excess. As with all events that involve alcohol, the organizers must provide drivers for those who become intoxicated.

PERMITS/LICENSES

Since a sport pool is considered gambling, check with the local law enforcement authorities, town clerk, or bureau of licensing to determine if a special state or county permit is required. If a party is planned, organizers must obtain the necessary food and drink permits.

HINTS

Although football is the sport most conducive to this type of pool, variations may be devised for other games that are scored, such as baseball and basketball. When the sport pool is combined with a party, the cost to the participants is significantly higher, as is the work involved on behalf of the organizers. Decide whether the additional profit justifies the extra work.

Mini Golf Putt-Putt
and Raffle

POTENTIAL NET INCOME

$1,500

COMPLEXITY/DEGREE OF DIFFICULTY

Low

DESCRIPTION

A valuable donated prize is raffled at an athletic contest or recreation activity. Raffle tickets for the prize may be obtained only by making a hole-in-one golf putt on a portable, homemade miniature golf platform. One attempt to make the somewhat difficult putt may be purchased for $1, or 7 attempts may be purchased for $5. If such a raffle is held at 15 athletic events throughout the season, the net profit can easily reach $1,500.

SCHEDULING

Each raffle and the accompanying putt-putt challenge may be conducted as part of an athletic or recreation event. The putt-putt activity is scheduled before the start of the accompanying event, then the raffle drawing is held during halftime or following the game or activity.

RESOURCES

Facilities: A portable, one-hole putt-putt platform must be constructed. This platform must be located close to the path of spectators who are walking to the accompanying event. Ideally, the platform is situated where a large group of spectators can view the participants as they attempt to make a hole-in-one. High foot traffic is a must.

Equipment and Supplies: Golf balls, putters, a cash box, tickets, signs, a public-address system, and a donated prize worth at least $100 are necessary.

Publicity and Promotion: On-site publicity is required to attract participants who are willing to donate $1 for each chance to win a raffle ticket that will make them eligible to win the prize. Use of the public-address system is very important. Signs should be prominently displayed within the facility, directing potential contestants to the site of the putt-putt activity. The sponsoring group might use the following sales pitch over the announcement system and on its posters: "Win a chance to win the big prize by making a hole-in-one putt!" Be sure to publicize and promote the fact that this is a fundraising effort. Let the public also know how the profits will be used by the nonprofit organization.

Time: This fundraising project can be planned and organized within a week. The portable putt-putt platform can be set up and taken down within minutes. Allow 60 minutes for the putt-putt contest to take place. The raffle for the prize can be drawn within a minute or two.

Expenditures: The putt-putt platform can be built from donated scrap wood and other materials. Golf balls and clubs can be obtained on a donated or loan basis. Allocate $50 for tickets and promotional materials. Have $50 in change on hand in the cash box.

Personnel (Staff and Volunteers): A few volunteers (3-5) and a small staff (1-2) are needed to handle the promotion of this combined activity, then oversee the putting and the raffle drawing. Additional influential supporters (2-3) are needed to solicit, on a donated basis, valuable items to be raffled at different athletic or recreation events.

RISK MANAGEMENT

There is no financial risk involved in this fundraising effort. To prevent injuries to contestants and spectators, organizers must ensure that golf clubs are not swung wildly or used in an otherwise dangerous manner. The organizers should emphasize that this is a putt-putt activity, not a 300-yard driving contest.

PERMITS/LICENSES

Check with the local municipal offices to determine whether a gambling or game-of-chance license is required in your community.

HINTS

If the putt-putt activity becomes very popular, the organizers may want to construct more than one platform so that more participants can putt within the time allotted. Potential donors should not have to wait in line too long for their turn at hitting the hole-in-one. The key to the success of this effort is securing desirable items to be raffled. Without valuable prizes, there would be no motivation for people to donate $1 (or more) for the opportunity to qualify for the drawing. Ideally, each prize should be worth at least $100.

Fall Birdseed Sale

POTENTIAL NET INCOME
$1,850

COMPLEXITY/DEGREE OF DIFFICULTY
Low

DESCRIPTION
Fifty-pound bags of various kinds of birdseed are sold on an advance-sale basis. The birdseed is priced to sell at a profit of $5 per bag, and the money is usually collected when the order is taken. At the time of ordering, purchasers are told when and where they are to pick up the birdseed. After all individual orders have been received, the sponsoring organization forwards the total order to the wholesaler. The bags of birdseed are delivered to a central location where individual purchasers are to pick up their orders on a specific day.

SCHEDULING
The advance orders for birdseed are taken in the early fall.

RESOURCES
Facilities: A central location is needed where the orders of birdseed may be delivered from the wholesaler and then distributed to the individual purchasers. There also is a need for a dry, rodent-free storage room or garage where unclaimed bags of birdseed can be stored until picked up.

Equipment and Supplies: Posters are necessary for publicity purposes. The salespersons need order forms, and a master order book is required to keep accurate records of the individual orders. A sign is helpful at the site where the bags are picked up.

Publicity and Promotion: This fundraiser is publicized throughout the community by announcements and advertisements in the area news media and through the display of posters in various business establishments. Some businesses and organizations also can serve as sites where advance orders may be taken. Many adults can take order forms to work and discreetly solicit orders from their coworkers, thus greatly increasing the pool of potential buyers. The organizers should retain the names, addresses, and phone numbers of all purchasers so that those people can be contacted when this fundraiser is held again.

Time: The sponsoring organization can plan this project and locate a suitable wholesaler within 2 weeks. The selling window should not exceed 4 weeks. Allow 7 to 10 days for the delivery of the birdseed from the wholesaler. The distribution of the bags to the individual purchasers should be scheduled on a Saturday between the hours of 10 A.M. and 4 P.M. For those bags that are not picked up on the appointed date (and there will always be some bags left unclaimed for numerous reasons), a second pickup date must be scheduled.

Expenditures: Allocate $150 to cover initial costs, which include promotional expenses. Payment to the wholesaler for the birdseed can be taken from the advance payments received from the customers.

Personnel (Staff and Volunteers): A large contingent of volunteers (35) and small staff (1-3) are needed to form the core of the sales team. Additional helpers (2-3) should be in charge of tallying the individual orders and submitting the total order to the wholesaler. Adult volunteers (4-5) should alternate attendance at the disbursement site to ensure that purchasers obtain the specific bags of birdseed that they ordered and paid for.

RISK MANAGEMENT

No hard-sell tactics are allowed. If children will be going door-to-door to take orders (and perhaps to collect the money), a training session must be conducted not only to teach them the correct selling techniques but also to explain the safety factors associated with selling on a door-to-door basis.

PERMITS/LICENSES

For door-to-door sales, many communities require that the sponsoring organization obtain a peddler's permit. Check with the town clerk or other municipal offices to determine whether your community has such a stipulation.

HINTS

The money for individual purchases of bags of birdseed should be collected when the order is taken. However, some organizations take orders and then collect the money when the bags are picked up. In the latter case, expect a 10 percent to 15 percent rate of people who will order birdseed but then not pick up the bags or pay for them.

All bags of birdseed must be picked up by the purchasers—there is (usually) no delivery. Some fundraising groups have delivered the bags to the homes of the purchasers (with payment made when the order is received). However, this can become very burdensome and complicated when, say, 400 bags of birdseed are ordered from the wholesaler on behalf of 125 individual purchasers.

Country Calendar and Cookbook Sale

POTENTIAL NET INCOME

$2,000

COMPLEXITY/DEGREE OF DIFFICULTY

Low

DESCRIPTION

Volunteers, boosters, and fans of a sponsoring organization sell country calendars and *A Taste of the Country* cookbooks. The calendars are sold for a profit of $3.50 each, and the cookbooks are sold for a profit of $5 each. Both items are created and printed by Reiman Publications in Greendale, Wisconsin (800-344-6913). The company provides free order forms, sample calendars, and a list of sales tips.

Volunteer salespersons are organized into teams. Selling can be done on either a take-order or point-of-sale ("show and sell") basis. With advance orders, the money can be collected at the time of the order or when the merchandise is delivered. Either way, the calendars and cookbooks must be delivered at a later date to each customer. Using the point-of-sale method requires that the organization order a number of calendars and cookbooks and then sell them "on the spot" to customers. This practice negates the need to make a second trip to deliver the merchandise. Donated prizes are awarded to the best sales teams.

SCHEDULING

This fundraiser can be started at any time of the year, although calendars are easiest to sell in October, November, and December. Door-to-door selling, however, is most successful in warm weather.

RESOURCES

Facilities: None

Equipment and Supplies: Cookbooks and calendars, order books, receipt books, and donated prizes are needed.

Publicity and Promotion: Announcements in local newspapers and advertising periodicals help to spread the word about this project. Highlight the fact that this is a fundraising effort sponsored by a worthy, nonprofit organization. Reveal how the profits will be used locally.

Time: This fundraiser can be planned within a week. Obtaining the needed information, order forms, and sample calendars and cookbooks from Reiman Publications can take another week or so. A selling window of no more than 2 weeks keeps the enthusiasm and friendly competition at a high level among the sales volunteers.

Expenditures: The cookbooks and calendars are paid for out of the money received from the sale of the items. Plan to spend $10 in promotional expenses to get this fundraiser started.

Personnel (Staff and Volunteers): A large group of volunteers (35-40) teamed with a small staff (1-2) can successfully complete this project. The greater the number of salespersons, the better. Both adults and youngsters can join the sales force. Parents can purchase the calendar and cookbook themselves and also sell to their coworkers, relatives, and friends. Youngsters can canvass the neighborhoods and approach their grandparents.

RISK MANAGEMENT

Schedule an orientation session for the sales force to help them sell the merchandise. Emphasize the safety factors that should be observed in door-to-door sales, such as traveling in pairs and not selling at night or in unfamiliar neighborhoods unless accompanied by an adult. The financial risks are minimal. Unsold cookbooks can be returned to Reiman as long as they are unopened and in mint condition.

PERMITS/LICENSES

A peddler's permit might be necessary in some communities if sales are to be made on a door-to-door basis. Check with the local municipal bureau of licensing or the town clerk.

HINTS

Both the calendars and cookbooks can be sold, or the organizers may choose between them.

Alumni Keepsake Publication

POTENTIAL NET INCOME

$2,000

COMPLEXITY/DEGREE OF DIFFICULTY

Moderate

DESCRIPTION

A sport or recreation organization publishes an alumni keepsake publication to be sold to alumni, supporters, and fans. The publication traces the history of the organization up to the present time and includes interesting stories and photographs depicting activities, programs, people, and facilities. The keepsake is sold at a price that generates a net profit of $10 each (or whatever the market will bear). If 200 copies are sold, the sponsoring organization nets $2,000.

SCHEDULING

The keepsake project can be initiated at any time. However, the timing of such a publication is enhanced when some special accomplishment or milestone of the organization is close at hand, such as its 50th or 100th anniversary.

RESOURCES

Facilities: No specific facility is required. Work on the book, including computer work, paste-ups, editing, and so forth, can take place at different offices donated for the specific amount of time needed to complete the task(s) at hand.

Equipment and Supplies: A computer, desktop publishing software, phones, order forms, display tables, stationery, envelopes, and stamps are required. A camera and film are needed to take current pictures for the publication.

Publicity and Promotion: Preselling the publication is a key factor in the financial success of this fundraiser. Send a mailing to all alumni announcing the availability of the book and stating its prepublication price. Explain that the price offered at that time is lower than it will be after publication and that there will be a limited number of the books available after a certain date. This encourages advance orders. Announcements also can be made, and orders taken, at other events sponsored by the sponsoring organization. At events that take place prior to the publication date, a mock-up of the book's cover is used to promote the keepsake. After the date of publication, unsold books are made available on display tables at functions of the organization and will remain available until sold out.

Time: The planning stage of this fundraising project can take less than 2 weeks. However, the time involved in working on the publication (e.g., collecting the data; organizing the contents; selecting the photographs; writing the copy) can take many months. Plan to spend 4 to 6 months of concentrated effort before seeing the book in print. During the time that the keepsake is being created, the efforts of staff and volunteers can be spent marketing and selling advance orders of the book. After it is in print, selling efforts will continue until all copies have been sold.

Expenditures: Even with the loan of a camera, computers, a laser printer, and desktop publishing software, a budget of $500 will be necessary to get the publication ready to go to press. An appropriate cover must be designed, and each copy must be bound. The final cost of the book will be affected significantly by how the book is bound (spiral, stitched, or hardcover), the type and color quality of the cover, the quality and quantity of the pages, and the number of photographs. Quick-service print shops can print and bind at minimal costs. Many businesses also have these capabilities and may be approached to print and bind the publications for free.

Personnel (Staff and Volunteers): Many volunteers (20-25) and a small staff (2-4) are involved in tracing the history of the organization, securing interesting stories, selecting copies of old photographs, interviewing people, and conducting other research. Some of these volunteers also can be involved in marketing, selling, and distributing of the finished product. One or more individuals skilled in editing and proofing manuscripts are invaluable to this project.

RISK MANAGEMENT

There is always a risk that incorrect information will get into print. Other types of errors (typographical, for instance) or omissions are certainly possible. Thus, it is imperative to find expert editors to review the various drafts and ensure that no grammatical or factual errors creep in and that no significant omissions occur. All photographs should be in good taste, and references to individuals must not be libelous. To reduce the financial risk involved in creating and printing a given number of books and then attempting to sell them, organizers should take advance orders as part of the promotion campaign. Then the sponsoring organization prints an additional 100 to 200 copies to sell on speculation.

PERMITS/LICENSES

None

HINTS

Every individual, or that person's family, whose name is in the publication is a candidate to buy a copy. Those whose photos are included are prime candidates.

Exam Care Packages for Students

POTENTIAL NET INCOME
$2,000

COMPLEXITY/DEGREE OF DIFFICULTY
Moderate

DESCRIPTION

The sponsoring organization sends to students' parents a letter and an order form that illustrate a variety of edible goodies that can be delivered to their children during the week of final exams. The promoters select from various wholesalers a variety of items that are conducive to eating quick snacks: soft drinks, candy and granola bars, cookies, crackers, jelly, apples, plastic eating utensils, and so forth. The order form should provide a selection of 4 or 5 care packages that contain different items and vary in price. Accompanying each package is an individual, computer-generated message from the parents. Each care package is priced to provide a net profit to the sponsoring organization of 60 percent of the selling price.

SCHEDULING

This fundraising project is a natural within an educational setting and can be implemented once at the end of the fall semester and again at the end of the school year.

RESOURCES

Facilities: A room is required to store the food and supplies. This can be the same room where volunteers put together the individual care packages.

Equipment and Supplies: A large number of cover letters, envelopes, and order blanks are needed for the mass mailing. Use of a computer, word processing software, and high-quality printer greatly facilitate the creation of the form letters and the individualized messages from the parents to the students. Volunteers donate their time and the use of their vehicles to deliver the care packages to the students, either at school or at home.

Publicity and Promotion: The letters to parents and the order blanks form the foundation of the publicity campaign surrounding this project. Publicize this fundraiser, and the purpose for which the money will be used, on various school and community bulletin boards and in newsletters and other publications. The care packages also can be marketed to the students themselves; that is, the students may order the packages for their boyfriends and girlfriends. This can be done through the school newspapers and via public-address announcements at the schools and at athletic events.

Time: The letters should be mailed approximately 4 to 5 weeks prior to the end of each semester. This allows sufficient time to receive the orders, fill the orders, and deliver the packages. All of the orders should be filled and delivered within a week.

Expenditures: The major expenses involve the postage for the mailings and the contents of the care packages. Plan to spend around $200 for mailing and advertising costs plus another $300 for the initial inventory of food and supplies (e.g., boxes, plastic utensils).

Personnel (Staff and Volunteers): A large number of volunteers (35-40) and a small staff (2-3) are necessary because all of the work is condensed into a short period of time.

RISK MANAGEMENT

The financial risks are minimal. The orders from parents and friends will contain the money (in the form of checks) needed to pay for the items to be purchased and delivered to the students. Since the orders all will come in around the same time, this can create a bottleneck in terms of being able to fill and deliver the individual orders on time. To head off this problem, the promoters must involve a large number of volunteers to pack the care packages and to deliver them to the individual students. Purchasing the items from legitimate vendors reduces the liability exposure on behalf of the fundraising entity since the food items all are professionally packaged and dated for freshness. Also, all unused and unopened food usually can be returned within a reasonable time to the wholesaler.

PERMITS/LICENSES

To deliver the care packages to students in elementary and secondary schools, the sponsoring organization must first obtain permission from the school authorities. Delivery is seldom a problem with college students. Outside vendors frequently deliver to students in dormitories and there is no need to obtain permission to deliver to students in rental housing.

HINTS

Each care package is accompanied by an envelope that contains a list of the package's contents and an individualized gift card identifying from whom the package was sent. Some sponsoring organizations also provide, for an additional cost, a singing-telegram service through which the recipient of the care package is serenaded with one of a number of predetermined songs.

Flag Day Sale

POTENTIAL NET INCOME

$2,400

COMPLEXITY/DEGREE OF DIFFICULTY

Low

DESCRIPTION

American flags (and flag holders) are sold prior to national Flag Day. Flags suitable for display outside of homes and businesses are sold throughout the community at a $10 profit. The flags can be sold on either a take-order or point-of-sale ("show and sell") basis. The sponsoring organization's goal is to sell 250 flags.

SCHEDULING

Because Flag Day is June 14, the sale of flags takes place in May and early June.

RESOURCES

Facilities: The sponsoring organization needs a site at which to store the flags and holders until all are sold.

Equipment and Supplies: Signs, flyers, receipt books, record books, flags, and flag holders are necessary. Donated prizes are given to the top sellers.

Publicity and Promotion: Advance publicity should be included in area newspapers and advertising periodicals. Due to the non-profit nature of this fundraiser, radio and television stations might provide free air time as part of their public-service announcements. Local businesses and organizations can display signs that promote the sale of the flags. Veteran groups and law enforcement agencies are prime candidates for sales and for free publicity and volunteer help. Don't hesitate to play upon the potential customers' patriotic feelings when marketing the flags. Use the public-address system at other events sponsored by the sport or recreation organization to promote this project. Highlight the fact that this fundraiser is sponsored by a local, nonprofit organization to help a worthy community cause.

Time: This simple yet highly effective fundraiser can be planned and organized within a week. It takes up to 3 weeks to receive the flags and holders after the order has been placed. Schedule 1 or more hours of training to teach youngsters and other volunteers the proper way to market and sell the flags. The selling window should not extend beyond 3 to 4 weeks. Almost all the flags that can be sold will be sold during this time period.

Expenditures: This fundraiser can be initiated for as little as $100. Although some wholesalers require advance payment for the entire cost of the flag order, others require only a partial down payment, with the remaining money due within 30 days. Others allow credit-worthy nonprofit organizations to delay any payment until 30 days after delivery, thus allowing more than enough time for the fundraising group to collect the money owed to the wholesaler.

Personnel (Staff and Volunteers): Many volunteers (35-45) and a small staff (1-2) form the core of the marketing and selling teams. Both youngsters and adults can sell the flags. Orders can be taken by parents at their place of work and from their friends and relatives.

RISK MANAGEMENT

No hard-sell tactics are allowed. Also instruct youngsters about the safety precautions to take when selling door-to-door. For example, they should not travel alone when soliciting sales, they should stay in familiar neighborhoods or be accompanied by an adult, and they should not solicit customers after dusk. There is always a danger in the take-order method of selling that the customers will not have the cash or will have moved or otherwise be unable to pay for the flags upon delivery. In this event, top sellers should be given an extra weekend during which to sell these flags.

PERMITS/LICENSES

If the flags are sold door-to-door, a peddler's permit might be required. Check with the municipal bureau of licenses or the town clerk.

HINTS

Be sure to deal with a reputable flag wholesaler. Get a firm commitment in terms of the delivery date of the flags. To make the selling process an exciting and enjoyable experience, organize the salespersons into competitive teams, then give donated prizes to the top individual sellers (according to age) and to the most successful teams.

The flags can be sold either on a take-order or point-of-sale ("show and sell") basis. In the take-order method, the sellers carry a sample flag to show customers and take the orders before the flags are purchased from the wholesaler. Using this method, the salesperson must make an extra trip back to the customer to deliver the flag. Some selling groups collect the money when the order is placed; others collect it upon delivery of the flag. If the money is collected at the time of ordering, there will be no danger of having unsold merchandise at the conclusion of the selling period. In the point-of-sale method, flags are on hand to give to the customer when the individual agrees to buy the flag. This eliminates the need to make a return trip to the customer but requires that an inventory of flags be purchased at the sponsoring organization's expense. Unsold flags should be stored in a safe place until the following year when this fundraising effort can be initiated again. There is always a market for new flags.

Screen-Printed Scarves for Sale

POTENTIAL NET INCOME

$2,450

COMPLEXITY/DEGREE OF DIFFICULTY

Moderate

DESCRIPTION

A schoolwide or community-wide art contest is held to determine the hand-painted pattern(s) to be screen printed on cotton neck scarves. The scarves are sold to the sponsoring organization's fans and supporters and to the general public. The scarves can be produced by the staff and volunteers or by a commercial silk screener. The price of each souvenir scarf is calculated to allow for an average net profit of $25 per. The goal is to sell 100 scarves on both a take-order and point-of-sale basis.

SCHEDULING

This fundraiser can be scheduled at any time of the year. However, if a special event has taken place, such as a championship being won, the creation of the special design for the scarves can commemorate this special event and should be timed accordingly.

RESOURCES

Facilities: The sponsors must secure a room where the contestants can display their art work and where the judges can announce the winner(s). If the staff and volunteers are to create and screen the scarves themselves, the organization must supply a room for this purpose.

Equipment and Supplies: If the scarves are to be printed by the sponsors, they must provide the screen-printing press, the screen itself, appropriate inks, and a supply of scarves. If the job is to be done by a professional silk screener, the sponsors supply only the scarves. Posters are necessary to promote both the art contest and the sale of scarves.

Publicity and Promotion: The sponsoring organization should attempt to take advance orders for as many scarves as possible, thus diminishing the possibility of having a large quantity of unsold merchandise. Announcements must be made to promote both the art contest and the sale of the scarves. Announcements in the area news media and the display of posters in local businesses can help get the word out in the community. Some businesses also can serve as outlets for the sale of the scarves, either before or after they have been printed.

Time: This fundraiser can be planned within 2 weeks. Four to 6 weeks notice should be given prior to the art contest to allow time for the completion of the paintings. The art can be set up in a few hours, and the judging can be completed in perhaps 3 hours, followed by the public announcement of the winner(s). The take-order selling window for the neck scarves should be 3 to 4 weeks. If scarves also are to be sold on a point-of-sale basis, there should be an additional selling window of 3 to 4 weeks.

Expenditures: Allocate $50 for promotional activities. The current price for unprinted cotton scarves is approximately $4 per. If the volunteers and staff print the scarves themselves, the sponsors must add approximately $1.50 to the price of the scarves; if the scarves are commercially printed, the added cost will be approximately $3.50 per.

Personnel (Staff and Volunteers): Several volunteers (15-20) and a small staff (1-2) are needed to market and sell the scarves on both a take-order and point-of-sale basis. Five judges are necessary for the art contest, and a master of ceremonies is useful if the announcement of the winner(s) is done at a public gathering, such as at an athletic contest or recreational activity.

RISK MANAGEMENT

The financial risk is reduced greatly if most of the selling is done through advance sales. However, even if a number of scarves are not sold within 5 weeks they can remain for sale until all have been purchased. Leftover scarves also can be given away as special gifts to boosters.

PERMITS/LICENSES

If the scarves are to be sold door-to-door, a peddler's permit might be necessary. Check with the town clerk or other municipal office for details.

HINTS

At the end of the time period allotted for the advance-order selling window, you can calculate where you stand on the organization's goal to sell 100 scarves. Generally speaking, two-thirds of the scarves will be sold through advance orders. The remaining one-third can be sold door-to-door.

When taking advance orders for scarves, the salespersons should show prospective customers a picture of the design so they can see how beautiful the finished product will be. Emphasize that this is a fundraising project conducted by a nonprofit entity and that all of the profits will be spent on a worthy cause within the community. Naturally, the many fans, boosters, and friends of the sponsoring organization are prime prospects to purchase the scarves.

If there is more than one winner in the art contest, there will be more than one design to be printed on the scarves. While this provides purchasers with a better selection, it also creates the possibility that one design might be more popular than the others, making the others harder to sell.

Lip Synch Contest

POTENTIAL NET INCOME

$2,350

COMPLEXITY/DEGREE OF DIFFICULTY

Low

DESCRIPTION

The organization holds a contest in which participants lip synch to popular songs. Both individual and group competitions are held. Categories of competition can be based on the type of songs being lip synched (e.g., rock and roll, country and western, oldies) and upon the ages of the participants. An entry fee of $45 is charged for each contestant or group. Individual prizes are presented for the best and most outrageous costumes in the various categories. Entry fees are paid by the individual contestants or by their sponsors. Tickets are sold (both in advance and at the door) to the event. Additional profits ($300) are realized through the sale of refreshments.

SCHEDULING

This fun event can be scheduled on almost any evening or on a Saturday or Sunday afternoon.

RESOURCES

Facilities: The contest can be held in any large room, such as an auditorium or gymnasium. The sponsors must provide a stage or other open area where the contestants can "strut their stuff" to the music in front of the audience. There must be room for the audience to be seated comfortably.

Equipment and Supplies: Tables, chairs, decorations, posters, a cash box, tape player or compact disc player, public-address system, concession items, and tickets are required. The prizes (ribbons, trophies, and gift certificates) to be awarded to the winners in the various categories are donated, as are some of the concession items to be sold.

Publicity and Promotion: Announcements should be included in the area newspapers and advertising periodicals. Highlight the nonprofit nature of the organizing group, and publicize how the profits will be put to good use within the community. Radio and television stations might promote this fundraising event as part of their public-service announcements. Use the public-address system at other events sponsored by the organizing group to publicize the upcoming lip synch contest. Display posters in area businesses and organizations to announce this fun contest. Some businesses also can serve as advance-sale ticket outlets. Be sure to note on the promotional posters the recording format participants must bring (CDs, tapes, or records).

Time: This fundraiser can be planned within a few days. Reserve the facility at least 4 to 6 months prior to the date of the contest. The advance publicity should last 3 to 4 weeks in order to allow the participants enough time to prepare for the competition and to solicit sponsorship donations. The lip synch contest itself lasts 3 to 5 hours, depending on the number of contestants.

Expenditures: Since the prizes and decorations are donated and all other items (including sound equipment) are loaned, the major expenses are related to the promotional aspects, renting the site (if this is not also donated for the event), and stocking the concession. Allocate $200 for total expenses, including the concession items.

Personnel (Staff and Volunteers): Several volunteers (15-20) and a small staff (1-2) are necessary to organize and implement this fundraising project. Helpers are needed to sell tickets, solicit free gifts, prepare the site, staff the concession stand, and clean up after the event. A colorful and entertaining master of ceremonies will help make the event enjoyable for the contestants and the audience. An impartial group of adult judges (4-5) is also needed.

RISK MANAGEMENT

Financial risk is kept to a minimum since there are advance ticket sales and almost all of the equipment and supplies are either donated or loaned. Liability exposure is minimal. Be sure to adhere to the health regulations pertaining to the storage, preparation, and dispensing of food and drink to the public. It's important to check the sound equipment before the event—you wouldn't want technical glitches to ruin the performances.

PERMITS/LICENSES

A concession permit might be required in some communities. Check with the health department or town clerk.

HINTS

For the net profit goal to be met, a large number of contestants must become involved in this event. Fifty participants will bring in $2,250 from entry fees alone. Be sure to publicize that the contests are for people of all ages—ranging from the very young to the very mature. In addition to individual contestants, businesses and organizations can submit team entries. The larger the number of contestants the better—in terms of both profit and fun.

15

Cashola Delight

POTENTIAL NET INCOME

$2,500

COMPLEXITY/DEGREE OF DIFFICULTY

Low

DESCRIPTION

Volunteers of the sponsoring organization sell "Cashola Delight" coupons (make-believe dollar bills) from a fast food restaurant. Each coupon buys a dollar's worth of food and drink at that particular restaurant. The group selling the coupons keeps 50 cents for every make-believe dollar sold. A group of 40 dedicated volunteers reasonably can be expected to sell over $5,000 worth of the coupons within a community.

SCHEDULING

This easy fundraising project can be held at any time of the year.

RESOURCES

Facilities: None

Equipment and Supplies: The Cashola Delight coupons are provided by the sponsoring entity. If prizes are to be given to the top salespersons, these gifts should to be solicited as donations from area businesses and organizations.

Publicity and Promotion: Announcements should be sent to the area newspapers, including the local advertising periodicals. Use the public-address system at other activities sponsored by the fundraising group to publicize the Cashola Delight project. When selling the coupons, the salespersons should make each prospective purchaser aware that one-half of the money raised will go to a worthy cause sponsored by the nonprofit group. Don't forget to emphasize that for every Cashola Delight "dollar" purchased, the individual can buy a dollar's worth of food or drink at the cooperating restaurant while helping your worthy group achieve its financial objective.

Time: The sponsoring organization can firm up the details of this fundraiser within 3 weeks. The selling window for the coupons should be limited to 4 to 5 weeks.

Expenditures: The seed money is $30 for the printing of the coupons.

Personnel (Staff and Volunteers): A large group of volunteers (40) and a small staff (1-2) are needed to blanket the community with the Cashola Delight "dollars."

RISK MANAGEMENT

There is no financial risk involved. In order to reduce the liability exposure, the sponsors should educate their salespersons— especially youngsters—in the area of safety. For example, children should obey traffic laws (no jaywalking), travel in pairs, and not sell at night or in strange neighborhoods without being accompanied by an adult. All salespersons should be taught how to politely solicit sales from potential customers. No hard-sell approaches are allowed.

PERMITS/LICENSES

A peddler's permit might be required in your community for door-to-door sales. Check with the town clerk, the bureau of licenses, or other municipal offices.

HINTS

This is a very easy and yet highly successful fundraising project. The success or failure of this project depends upon the number of salespersons and how effective they are in selling the Cashola Delight coupons. Many of the sponsoring organizations give prizes (donated from local merchants) to the top individual sellers, thereby adding to their motivation to reach high sales figures. Other sponsors organize the salespersons into teams and then provide prizes for the top-selling groups as well as to the top individual salespersons.

If people understand that they are purchasing a dollar's worth of merchandise for a dollar in real money while also helping a worthy local organization reach important goals, there is a high likelihood of financial success. Don't forget to thank publicly the cooperating restaurant that enabled your organization to execute this fundraising project.

Value Rummage Sale

POTENTIAL NET INCOME

$2,500

COMPLEXITY/DEGREE OF DIFFICULTY

Moderate

DESCRIPTION

Donated new and used items of value are sold at bargain prices. This is not a junkyard or garage sale. Items of worth (e.g., furniture, bikes, lawn equipment) are sold at bargain prices.

SCHEDULING

This fundraising project can stand alone or be scheduled in conjunction with an athletic contest or recreation event. The sale can be held one time, or it can be scheduled annually or biannually at almost any time of the year as long as the weather is good. If held outdoors, plan for a rain date or use a tent to provide shelter. The event can be scheduled at the organizing group's facility or at a site donated for this purpose.

RESOURCES

Facilities: Location is all-important to this fundraiser because vehicular and foot traffic must be substantial. The indoor or outdoor facility must be large enough to adequately display the items for sale. Ample parking space also must be available. The sponsoring organization provides a place to store the donated items until the time of the rummage sale and afterward to store unsold goods if there is to be another sale. If another sale is not planned, leftover merchandise usually is given to charity.

Equipment and Supplies: Tables for the display of sale items are needed, and signs must be created. A cash box, $100 in change, a receipt book, and a record book must be on hand. The group creates promotional posters and flyers. A tent or tarpaulin must be available in the event of inclement weather. A first-aid kit should be on hand.

Publicity and Promotion: Announcements in local advertising periodicals and other print media are essential. Word-of-mouth promotional efforts can be very effective, as can flyers distributed within the community and posters displayed in the windows of area businesses. On the weekend of the rummage sale, there should be signs around the site identifying the location of the sale.

There are two distinct components of publicity involved in promoting the Value Rummage Sale. First, the organizing group must solicit people and businesses to donate new and used items for this worthwhile project. Second, the group must attract a sufficient number of potential buyers. During your promotional efforts, be sure to mention some of the most impressive items to be on sale.

Time: Planning for the event can be concluded within a week. The solicitation, collection, and storage of donated items can take as long as 2 to 4 months and might even exist on a continuing basis throughout the year. The sale starts at 5 P.M. on a Friday afternoon and runs through Sunday until 4 P.M. Cleanup activities will consume 2 to 3 hours.

Expenditures: All items to be sold are obtained free from boosters, fans, members of the general public, and merchants. This fundraiser can be initiated for less than $50, to be spent for advertising and signs.

Personnel (Staff and Volunteers): A small staff (1-5) and an extensive number of volunteers (40-45) are needed to find items that might be obtained from contributors. This group also transports the goods to the site of the rummage sale and staffs the event on a rotating basis. A person trained in first aid and CPR should be on hand.

RISK MANAGEMENT

There is no financial risk because all sale items are donated. Ensure that the owners of the site have adequate insurance coverage in the event of an accident or injury.

PERMITS/LICENSES

A permit might be required in some communities for a rummage sale. There might be specific requirements in terms of meeting community or municipal regulations regarding parking, sanitation, and availability of drinking water. Check with the city offices or town clerk.

HINTS

All promotional activities should highlight the worthiness of the sponsoring group, the purpose for which the money raised will be used, and the numerous bargains to be found in the quality goods at the sale. Promoting some of the nicest offerings (perhaps a weekend escape at the Holiday Inn, a previously owned 10-speed bicycle, or a new lawn mower) will generate interest and attract more customers. Be sure to thank (publicly, if possible) those who donated goods for the sale. For new merchandise, place the name of the donor on a card next to the item. Acknowledging the donors is important because you might want to ask for their help again. Don't allow the salespersons to sell to close associates, friends, or supporters prior to the official start of the rummage sale. This would alienate the general public and others who were not given such preferential treatment. Besides, all of the good stuff might be gone before the start of the sale!

Family-Style Pork Supper

POTENTIAL NET INCOME

$2,500

COMPLEXITY/DEGREE OF DIFFICULTY

Moderate

DESCRIPTION

A delicious dinner consisting of generous cuts of ham, scalloped potatoes, coleslaw, applesauce, green beans with bacon, rolls, a variety of drinks, and homemade deserts is provided. Tickets are $7 for adults and $3.50 for children under 11 years of age. (These prices might have to be adjusted for your community.) Tickets are available both in advance and at the door.

SCHEDULING

The Family-Style Pork Supper can be scheduled on any Friday or Saturday evening.

RESOURCES

Facilities: The sponsoring organization provides a site that will accommodate 150 to 300 diners at one time. A school cafeteria, a large recreational meeting room, or even a gymnasium (with the floors covered with tarpaulin) can be used. The room should be obtained at little or no cost. Adequate parking, close to the facility, should be available. Ideally, the site should be conveniently located for the patrons.

Equipment and Supplies: Donated food and drink; paper napkins, tablecloths, plates, and cups; and plastic utensils are all required. Signs, flyers, markers, tables, chairs, a public-address system, pots and pans for cooking, and food warmers also are necessary. A tarpaulin is necessary if the floor of the facility needs to be protected.

Publicity and Promotion: Announcements can be displayed in local newspapers and advertising periodicals and in any publications sponsored by the organizing group. All of the necessary information (e.g., the date, time, cost) must be included in the promotions. Public-address announcements can be made at community athletic contests or recreation events. In some communities, radio and television stations may provide free publicity for the dinner as part of their public-service announcements. Signs can be displayed throughout the community at the sites of different businesses and organizations, some of which can sell advance tickets. Flyers can be placed on parked vehicles at area malls and shopping centers. Promote the fact that this is a fundraising event sponsored by a local nonprofit organization, and specifically state how the profits will be spent.

Time: This project can be organized within 2 weeks. However, the group may need 4 weeks to ascertain who will be donating the necessary items and services for this project. Confirm the availability of the site at least 6 months prior to the event. Plan for 3 to 4 weeks of advance publicity. Allow 3 to 4 hours to set up the facility for the dinner. The time period for the meal (served continuously) is from 5:30 P.M. until around 10 P.M. Cleanup activities will take 1 to 2 hours.

Expenditures: This fundraising project will require $200 in seed money. All food and drink should be obtained free or at cost. The facility should be obtained gratis due to the nonprofit nature of the event.

Personnel (Staff and Volunteers): Many volunteers (20-25) and a small staff (1-2) are necessary to plan and implement this fundraising effort. Helpers solicit donations of food and drink, sell and collect tickets, cook and dispense the food, and so forth.

RISK MANAGEMENT

Selling advance tickets provides the organizers with an idea of the number of people who will attend the event; 73 percent to 80 percent of the total meals served will be through tickets sold in advance. The financial risk is greatly diminished if there is adequate advance publicity. Liability exposure is reduced if all of the health and safety regulations are strictly obeyed. Cooks and servers of the food should wear plastic gloves and their hair should be tied back. The dining area should be kept spotless, and the tables should be cleared as soon as the patrons have finished eating their dinners.

PERMITS/LICENSES

If the dinner is not held at a licensed eating establishment, the sponsoring group may need to obtain a temporary food permit or restaurant license. Check with the health department, the town clerk, or the local municipal licensing bureau. Be sure to obtain permission from the managers at the malls and shopping centers before placing flyers on vehicles parked in their lots.

HINTS

Reservations are suggested but not required. Carry-out orders may be taken. Once this fundraising project proves to be a success, subsequent Family-Style Pork Suppers will be even more popular and more financially rewarding. Some organizers give donated prizes to selected patrons (chosen at random) who are in attendance.

Youth Soccer Tournament

POTENTIAL NET INCOME
$2,500

COMPLEXITY/DEGREE OF DIFFICULTY
Moderate

DESCRIPTION
The sponsoring organization provides a round-robin or double-elimination tournament for young soccer enthusiasts, with 8 or 16 teams participating. Individual prizes and team trophies are awarded. To add to the educational value of the project, the sponsoring organization holds soccer clinics and workshops on the afternoon or evening prior to the tournament: one clinic for the youngsters, one for current and would-be coaches, and one for the parents. Profits are generated from the entry fees for each team ($25 to $50, or whatever the market will bear), the sale of concession items ($400-$600), and donations from individual sponsors and businesses ($1,200-$1,500).

SCHEDULING
The tournament can be scheduled on any weekend when good weather is expected. A rain date should be publicized in advance.

RESOURCES
Facilities: The organizing group reserves suitable playing fields. Adequate parking must be available.

Equipment and Supplies: The group obtains ribbons and trophies on a donated basis. Soccer balls, goals, tables, chairs, bleachers, posters, 35-millimeter camera and film, flyers, an outdoor public-address system, first-aid kits, portable phones, and portable scoreboards are necessary. Youngsters can wear their own uniforms, or the organizers can provide different-colored jerseys.

Publicity and Promotion: Display signs throughout the community to promote this educational, recreational, and fun event. Publicize how the profit will be put to good use. All of the local schools and youth organizations should receive information sheets that explain how teams can be entered in the tournament. News releases should be sent to the local news media and mention should be made in local advertising periodicals.

Time: The tournament can be organized within 2 weeks. Reserve the outdoor facility as early as possible—certainly before any publicity is released regarding the tournament. Allow 6 weeks for promotional efforts. Advance registration can be limited to 2 to 3 weeks. The tournament starts at 8 A.M. on a Saturday and continues through early Sunday evening. Plan to spend up to 2 hours setting up for the games at the start of each day and an hour cleaning up each day.

Expenditures: If the organizers are successful in soliciting contributions of cash, goods, and services, this fundraising project can be initiated with as little as $400 for publicity and for the initial concession inventory.

Personnel (Staff and Volunteers): Volunteer officials are a must. One or more volunteers trained in sports injuries (e.g., physician, nurse, certified trainer) should be in attendance. Many volunteers (25-30) and a small staff (1-2) are needed to organize the event, staff the concession stand, plan the publicity, and solicit sponsors.

RISK MANAGEMENT

Although soccer can be played in the rain, do not hesitate to use the rain date if the weather or field conditions are poor. On rainy days, beware of lightning and be sure that the fields are safe for play. It is better to postpone the competition than to endanger the youngsters. There is little financial risk involved because advance team registration (including the payment of entry fees) and the business and individual sponsorships ensure a profit. The games may be modified in terms of the time period allotted for each game, the stipulation that each member of the team play so many minutes, and so forth. Such rules reduce the likelihood that individual players will become overexerted and thus prone to injury. Having qualified officials work the games and medical personnel on hand also helps to diminish the liability risks.

PERMITS/LICENSES

Check with the local town clerk or health department to see if a license or permit is needed for the concession stand.

HINTS

The three workshops are held simultaneously and are made available to everyone in the area. They can be quite effective in promoting the project. The media might print information about the workshops and therefore provide more publicity about the youth tournament itself. The sponsoring organization should arrange to have photographs taken of the outstanding teams and individuals after the tournament is over. These pictures are sent to the local newspapers for possible inclusion in a follow-up story about the successful tournament/fundraising event. The group can give individual and team awards for such categories as "most improved," "outstanding sportsmanship," and so forth. This type of event can be planned and organized around almost any youth sport.

Peek-a-Boo Auction

POTENTIAL NET INCOME
$3,000

COMPLEXITY/DEGREE OF DIFFICULTY
Moderate

DESCRIPTION
This fundraising event features bidding for items that are not specifically identified either in terms of their exact value or even in respect to what they are. The items to be auctioned are disguised by placing them inside bags or by otherwise concealing them. Large objects can be hidden behind partitions while being auctioned. The unveiling of the items purchased by the successful bidders lends greatly to the excitement and suspense of the event.

The patrons are, however, given an idea or "peek" (hence the name Peek-a-Boo Auction) of the approximate value of what is to be auctioned, and are told the category of goods into which the item or service falls. This is accomplished by dividing the goods into general categories (e.g., certificates for services, tangible objects) and then subcategorizing them (e.g., clothing, recreational equipment, tickets). The general dollar value (e.g., $50-$100) of the item or service also is indicated. The major idea behind this type of auction is that the bidders really do not know what they are bidding on, having been given only a "peek" into its identity and value.

SCHEDULING
This type of auction can stand alone or can be combined with some other activity, such as a dinner affair, an athletic event, or a regular auction.

RESOURCES
Facilities: Almost any large room or outdoor space will suffice. There also is need for a site where the items to be auctioned can be stored.

Equipment and Supplies: All of the equipment and supplies associated with auctions can be provided by the professional auctioneer who runs the event. An excellent public-address system , including a portable microphone, and adequate tables and chairs are needed.

Publicity and Promotion: Announcements in the local news media are a must. Word-of-mouth communication can be effective. Distribute flyers and place posters in area businesses. As with all fundraising efforts for a good cause, the objective—to raise money for the youth baseball teams' uniforms or for the new ice-skating rink—should be highlighted.

Time: The number of items to be auctioned and the speed of the bidding largely will determine the length of the auction. Two to 4 hours is common for a stand-alone auction.

Expenditures: All items to be auctioned are donated. Even the services of the auctioneer can be obtained pro bono. Allot $100 for advertising expenses.

Personnel (Staff and Volunteers): A professional auctioneer is an absolute must. Several volunteers (10-15) and a small staff (1-2) of the sponsoring organization can assist in various roles, such as bookkeepers or as spotters for the auctioneer. There also is the need for 35 to 40 helpers to solicit, organize, and store the items that will be auctioned.

RISK MANAGEMENT

The risks of this fundraising event are centered around whether there are sufficient bidders in attendance and upon the quality and number of items to be auctioned. Effective publicity is the key to success. A captive audience is guaranteed when this auction is combined with another event, such as a dinner or athletic contest. The financial risk is negligible. Be sure that the blanket insurance coverage of the auction site will cover this activity. If not, you should obtain a special 1-day or event rider.

PERMITS/LICENSES

Special permits usually are not required if the auction is held on the site of the sponsoring organization. Check with the town clerk in the community in which the auction will take place. If a professional auctioneer is involved, this individual will be familiar with such requirements.

HINTS

A twist to this fundraising event is to have a swap session during or following the auction. In this way, the successful bidders can trade the items and services that they purchased. If the auction is not held in conjunction with a food event, a concession stand would be a profitable addition to this project.

PART II

FUNDRAISERS GENERATING FROM $3,000 TO $5,000

20

All-Star Circus

POTENTIAL NET INCOME

$3,450

COMPLEXITY/DEGREE OF DIFFICULTY

Low

DESCRIPTION

The sponsoring organization contacts a traveling circus to perform locally. Two 90-minute shows involve over a dozen circus acts. One such traveling group is Billy Martin's All-Star Circus, 103 Richmond Avenue, Olean, New York 14760 (716-372-1466). Some of the acts in this circus group have included Angela, a trapeze performer; the Bertinis, Czechoslovakian unicycle champions; Sir George, a tightwire artist; Abra the Clown; and a Wild West revue. Another traveling circus is the Frazen Brothers Circus, P.O. Box 1005, Webster, FL 33597 (800-234-6589 or 352-568-1854).

Adult admission is $6, with up to 2 accompanying children admitted free. The sponsoring organization derives the major portion of its profit from 40 percent of the gross ticket sales, with the circus organization retaining 60 percent of the gross ticket sales and 100 percent of souvenir sales. All concession profit is retained by the sponsoring organization. If 2,000 patrons attend the shows, and one-third of those are adults, the organization's take of the gross ticket sales would be $1,600. If each of those 2,000 patrons spends $1.50 at the concession stand, the additional net profit would be $2,000.

SCHEDULING

The circus can be scheduled for any Friday or Saturday night. Some traveling circuses plan for a weekend of activities (Friday and Saturday) with two shows per day.

RESOURCES

Facilities: Any large indoor facility, such as a gymnasium or field house, will suffice. Or the circus may elect to set up its big top (tent) on any open field; some of these tents can accommodate 1,500 people. Free and safe parking is necessary.

Equipment and Supplies: The circus provides the equipment and supplies necessary for its acts (portable lights and sound system) and promotional items (e.g., souvenirs, posters, flyers). The sponsoring organization can provide tickets and additional posters and flyers. Cash boxes and concession inventory and equipment are also required.

Publicity and Promotion: Although the circus handles most of the publicity, the sponsoring group might want to display additional signs at area business sites. Some businesses and organizations could serve as locations for advance tickets. Extensive mention within the area news media, including advertising periodicals, is a must. This event is promoted and advertised as a true family experience sponsored by a well-known nonprofit organization, with the profit going to a worthwhile cause within the community.

Time: Planning for this event will take 2 weeks. However, the circus group and site may have to be reserved up to 12 months in advance. Allow 3 hours for the circus personnel to set up the facility and another 2 hours to remove the equipment. Each circus show consists

of over 90 minutes of fast-paced action. Allow 45 minutes between shows to empty the facility.

Expenditures: Allocate $1,000 for initial concession inventory. Another $150 will go toward printing the tickets, promoting the event, and hiring a security guard. Payment for the services of the circus will be paid out of the ticket sales.

Personnel (Staff and Volunteers): Many volunteers (20-25) and a few staff members (2-4) are needed to promote the circus and sell advance tickets. Additional helpers (10-15) are needed to organize and staff the concession stand. Adult supervisors (5-6) and at least one security guard should be on site throughout the production.

RISK MANAGEMENT

The circus organization provides insurance that absolves the sponsors from liability in case of accidents that occur because of the circus. Check with the sponsoring organization's insurance company to confirm that you are adequately protected from liability exposure. If the site for the circus is indoors, the organizers should place a tarp on the floor for protection. If the event is to be held outdoors, be sure that the circus has a big top.

PERMITS/LICENSES

A concession permit or food license may be necessary. Check with the health department, the town clerk, or other municipal offices in your community.

HINTS

The circus personnel set up the facility, then take it down and clean up. The major responsibilities of the sponsoring group are to provide an adequate site, sell tickets, and staff the concession stand.

Lift-a-Thon

POTENTIAL NET INCOME

$3,500

COMPLEXITY/DEGREE OF DIFFICULTY

Low

DESCRIPTION

This fundraiser involves a weight-lifting exhibition in which youngsters in any sport perform three lifts: the bench press, the dead lift, and the squat. Prior to the event, each student solicits pledges from individuals and businesses, the amount of which is based on the total weight that the athlete will be able to lift using the three methods. The donors are assured of a cap on their financial obligations. For example, a donor might pledge $1.50 for each 50 pounds of total weight lifted by the individual, stipulating a maximum contribution of $25. The weight-lifting exhibition can stand alone or be held in conjunction with another sport or recreation activity.

SCHEDULING

The weight-lifting demonstration can be scheduled any weekend evening or afternoon.

RESOURCES

Facilities: The organization should attempt to secure a large weight room or gymnasium, but any open room that will accommodate the weight lifters and spectators will suffice. If a gymnasium is used, pad the floor so that the weights will not damage the surface.

Equipment and Supplies: Posters and pledge forms are needed. Weight benches, weights, barbells, a large blackboard (to record results), chalk, tables, chairs, towels, drinking bottles, protective rubber padding for the floor, a first-aid kit, and a public-address system are necessary.

Publicity and Promotion: Place announcements in area newspapers and advertising periodicals. Local radio and television stations might make public-service announcements. Businesses and organizations can display posters. Be sure to relate in all publicity efforts that the sponsoring organization is a nonprofit entity, and highlight how the profits will be used.

Time: This project can be planned within a week. The solicitation period for pledges should be limited to a maximum of 4 weeks. An orientation session for those to be involved in the Lift-a-Thon can be completed within 3 hours. The weight-lifting demonstration may take 4 hours. Allow 3 hours to set up the facility and an additional hour for cleanup. Collection of the pledges can be completed over a weekend.

Expenditures: This fundraiser can be initiated for less than $100, most of which is for promotional efforts.

Personnel (Staff and Volunteers): Fifteen to 25 youngsters are needed to solicit pledges and participate in the weight lifting. Several adult volunteers (10-15) and a small staff (1-2) can plan and implement this fundraiser. Some of the volunteers will serve as spotters. A physician or athletic trainer should be present. A knowledgeable announcer is needed to explain the lifts as they are being performed.

RISK MANAGEMENT

There is little financial risk involved in this fundraiser. Anticipate a 10 percent to 12 percent difference between what is pledged and what will be collected. Liability exposure and the risk of physical injury to the weight-lifting participants are kept to a minimum if the organizers ensure that all potential lifters are properly trained in executing the different lifts and if qualified spotters are present. If the weight lifters are juveniles, they must be prevented from attempting to lift poundage that they have not successfully lifted in the past. Youngsters must secure permission from their parents prior to participating in the weight-lifting activities.

PERMITS/LICENSES

If pledges are to be solicited door-to-door, a peddler's permit may be necessary. Check with the town clerk or other municipal offices.

HINTS

The training session for the participants in this event covers the appropriate tactics for soliciting pledges and the safety measures that must be followed while executing the different lifts. After the exhibition, the sponsoring group provides each athlete with a formal statement that verifies the total weight lifted by the individual; this document also thanks the donors for their support. The athlete shows the statement when collecting the pledges. A list of the contributors should be printed in one of the nonprofit group's publications and could also be displayed on a bulletin board in a facility for several months following the Lift-a-Thon.

Daffodil and Tulip Bulb Sale

POTENTIAL NET INCOME

$3,500

COMPLEXITY/DEGREE OF DIFFICULTY

Low

DESCRIPTION

Volunteers go door-to-door to solicit orders for daffodil and tulip bulbs. When all of the individual orders are in, the organizers send the purchase order to the wholesaler. After the bulbs have been received, they are picked up by the individual purchasers at a central location on a specified date. Although the sponsoring organization may obtain the money when the purchasers pick up the bulbs, payment is best received when the order is initially taken.

SCHEDULING

The selling process should begin no later than the first week in September.

RESOURCES

Facilities: The group needs a site where the bulbs can be delivered from the wholesaler and then stored until picked up by the individual purchasers.

Equipment and Supplies: Signs, order forms, and receipt books are necessary. Color flyers (obtained from the wholesaler) show prospective purchasers the beautiful flowers that will bloom from the bulbs. If some of the purchasers will be paying for their orders at the time of pickup, a cash box with change will be needed at the site.

Publicity and Promotion: Display posters at area businesses and organizations, some of which may accept orders and money for the sponsoring group. The local media might mention this fundraising project as part of their public-service announcements. Use public-address systems at community events to publicize the bulb sale. A training session should be held to teach salespersons the proper approach for selling. The sales pitch is that customers will not only receive value for their money but will help the sponsoring organization earn much-needed funds to pay for worthwhile activities within the community.

Time: This project can be planned within a day or two, although arrangements with a bulb wholesaler may take up to a week. The selling window is 2 to 3 weeks. The bulbs usually arrive within 10 days of the purchase order, then can be picked up by the individual purchasers on a Saturday or Sunday between the hours of 1 and 4 P.M. For those who do not pick up their bulbs on the scheduled date, a second date must be arranged.

Expenditures: Plan to spend less than $100 for signs, advertising flyers, and order forms. The wholesaler is paid out of the money collected when taking the orders.

Personnel (Staff and Volunteers): A large group of volunteers (40-50) and a small staff (1-2) are needed to sell the bulbs. Additional helpers (4-7) are necessary to organize and promote the project and to give the bulbs to purchasers at the distribution site.

RISK MANAGEMENT

The financial risks are minimal because the order for the bulbs from the wholesaler is based on the number of individual orders. Liability exposure is reduced if the training session educates volunteers about the safety factors involved when selling door-to-door. For example, youngsters should not sell at night or in unfamiliar neighborhoods without the presence of an adult. They must obey all traffic laws—that is, they must not jaywalk or cross an intersection against the light—and should wear a reflective vest if selling after dusk.

PERMITS/LICENSES

Check with the local town clerk or other municipal offices to learn if a peddler's permit is necessary in your community.

HINTS

Wholesalers are listed in the yellow pages. For the sake of the sponsoring group's reputation, be sure that the bulbs are reasonably priced and of high quality. If the money is not collected when the orders are taken, anticipate that 10 percent to 12 percent of the purchasers will not show up to claim or pay for the bulbs. These unsold bulbs should be taken door-to-door in an effort to sell them. To expand the sales territory, adults may solicit orders from coworkers and friends outside the community; in such cases, the sellers may have to deliver the bulbs themselves.

Trip Packages to a Professional Sport Contest

POTENTIAL NET INCOME

$3,520

COMPLEXITY/DEGREE OF DIFFICULTY

Moderate

DESCRIPTION

Tickets to a professional sport contest are obtained for free or at a reduced cost and then sold as part of a package that includes a bus ride to and from the game site and a tailgate party prior to the game. These packages are sold in advance and are priced to generate $40 net profit per person. Two busloads of 44 passengers each would net the sponsoring group $3,520.

SCHEDULING

The excursion can be planned for any day when a professional team is scheduled to play and a block of tickets is available to the sponsoring group. Weekends are the most popular days for this event.

RESOURCES

Facilities: The sponsoring group must determine a central location where the buses will pick up and drop off the spectators. Secure parking must be available for those who wish to leave their vehicles at the bus site.

Equipment and Supplies: Food, drink, and portable cooking grills are needed for the tailgate party, as well as disposable plates, cups, napkins, and utensils.

Publicity and Promotion: The trip/ticket package may be promoted either as a family affair or as an adult-only event. Businesses and organizations may display posters and give out flyers. Word-of-mouth and individual solicitation of potential patrons is essential. The media may provide free publicity due to the nonprofit nature of the organizing group. Throughout the marketing and selling campaign, emphasize how the youngsters will benefit as a result of the profits from this excursion. Sales pitches will be particularly effective with boosters of the sponsoring organization and with acquaintances and friends of the people selling the tickets.

Time: Promoters should begin to plan this fundraising project as soon as the home-game schedule is announced by the professional team. Marketing begins 60 days prior to the game, and the selling window can extend from 3 to 4 weeks.

Expenditures: Allot $200 for promotional purposes. Other expenses include the tickets; buses and drivers; stadium parking; food and drink; disposable plates, cups, napkins, and utensils; and fuel for the grills. Many of those services and items might be donated, borrowed, or obtained at reduced cost. Allocate up to $300 for goods and services that cannot be obtained gratis.

Personnel (Staff and Volunteers): Several volunteers (15-20) and a small staff (1-2) can comprise an effective sales force if properly motivated and put in touch with promising prospects. Tap influential persons to sell the packages to businesses and organizations.

RISK MANAGEMENT

The professional team should specify a cut-off date by which the organization can return unsold tickets without incurring any cost. This diminishes the financial risk of the sponsoring group. Income from advance sales can be used to pay for remaining financial obligations. Liability exposure is minimal because the bus company's blanket insurance policy will protect against claims resulting from injuries on the buses. Make advance arrangements with the stadium authorities as to where the buses can be parked and where the tailgate party will be allowed.

PERMITS/LICENSES

No permits normally are required if the food is to be cooked and distributed at the site of a professional stadium. Check with the stadium management.

HINTS

This type of fundraiser is particularly effective in those communities that are within 4 hours' driving time of a home site of a professional team. Both day and overnight excursions can be planned. Although greater expenses and effort are involved with overnight trips, the package prices can be raised to garner perhaps a $75 net profit per person. This project also can be held for big-time university games. Tickets might be more readily available from those teams that do not sell out at every home game. However, if tickets are too readily available to the promoters due to the lackluster attraction of the game, these tickets may be difficult to sell as part of a package.

24

Bed Race

POTENTIAL NET INCOME

$4,000

COMPLEXITY/DEGREE OF DIFFICULTY

Moderate

DESCRIPTION

A fun-filled afternoon of games and contests is scheduled for adults and youngsters. The activities are centered around the bed races, which involve teams pushing beds along a racecourse. Each team consists of four pushers plus one person sitting on the bed. Awards are given to the race winners and for the best individual and group costumes and best bed decorations. The entry fee for each team is $150. The goal is to attract at least 20 teams. Additional profits are generated from a concession stand and perhaps from charging an admission fee of $2 for adults and $1 for school-age children. In addition to the bed races, other entertaining events are held throughout the afternoon for spectators as well as for members of the racing teams. These might include leaky-bedpan races, tug-of-wars, balloon tosses, pie-eating contests, and various relay races (e.g., spoon-and-egg races, three-legged races).

SCHEDULING

This outdoor event can be scheduled for any Saturday or Sunday when excellent weather is expected. Publicize a rain date should the weather turn bad.

RESOURCES

Facilities: A paved outdoor area, such as a parking lot, is ideal. The site could be at a school, recreation center, or mall. A public road might be closed for the activities and serve as a racecourse. If admission is charged, the site must be arranged in a way that will prevent gate-crashers from seeing the activities for free.

Equipment and Supplies: Decorated beds on wheels and protective bicycle headgear are provided by the individual racing teams. The organizing group provides posters, tickets, an outdoor public-address system, stopwatches, tables, traffic cones, and first-aid supplies. Depending upon what other activities are held, supplies such as bedpans, spoons, eggs, balloons, and so forth are necessary. The concession inventory must be provided. The group might also sell hats and T-shirts.

Publicity and Promotion: Businesses, organizations, and individuals are encouraged to enter teams in the bed races. Announcements should be included in area newspapers and advertising periodicals. Radio and television spots might be provided as part of the stations' public-service announcements. Place posters at the sites of various businesses and organizations.

Time: This fundraiser can be planned within 2 weeks. Reserve the site early. Allow 5 weeks to solicit a sufficient number of racing teams; collect their entry fees in advance. Preparation on the day of the event will take 2 to 3 hours. The afternoon festivities officially start at noon and conclude around 5 P.M. Cleanup can take 2 hours.

Expenditures: Allocate $100 for promotional and publicity materials. Team trophies and individual awards (small plaques and ribbons), if not donated, will cost less than $200. Allocate $100 for concessions. Everything else required for this fundraising project can be borrowed or obtained through donation.

Personnel (Staff and Volunteers): An athletic trainer, nurse, or physician should be present in case of accident or illness. Other volunteers (20-25) and staff (1-2) are needed to sell tickets, solicit entry teams, take tickets at the gate, construct the racecourse, staff the concession stand, and clean up after the event.

RISK MANAGEMENT

The financial risks are minimal because the entry fees are collected in advance. The greatest risk involves potential injuries to the racing team members, especially those who ride the beds. Racing team members are required to wear protective headgear. Participants should sign an agreement that absolves the sponsoring organization from liability.

PERMITS/LICENSES

A concession permit might be required in some communities. Check with the town clerk or bureau of licensing. Obtain advance permission to use the parking lot or road.

HINTS

Encourage the racing teams to adorn their beds with signs and decorations. Businesses and organizations may place advertising or sponsorship signs on their beds. Encourage spirited competition among businesses (e.g., real estate companies, banks, restaurants). The racecourse can be a straightaway or an obstacle course. If there are too many teams to have all compete at once, the organizers can run heats of 3 to 4 teams, with the best 5 or 6 competing in a race-off for the championship. Don't forget to provide a summary of the day's activities, including the winners of the races, to the news media.

Pie Toss

POTENTIAL NET INCOME

$4,000

COMPLEXITY/DEGREE OF DIFFICULTY

Low

DESCRIPTION

Opportunities to throw "pies," consisting of paper plates and whipped cream, at local celebrities are sold for $2 each or three tries for $5 at various times throughout the year. The pies are thrown from 10 feet to 15 feet at their target. This easy fundraising project can be piggy-backed with any number of other events sponsored by the organizing group.

SCHEDULING

The Pie Toss can be scheduled for both 1 hour before and 1 hour after other activities, and during halftime if the activities are athletic contests. Schedule 2 or more volunteers to serve, on a rotating basis, as the targets of the pies at each pie toss event.

RESOURCES

Facilities: Any area measuring 15 feet by 10 feet and located near the event facility will suffice. To attract potential patrons, the site must have heavy foot traffic.

Equipment and Supplies: The sponsoring organization supplies posters, a stool for the celebrities, plastic sheets to place around the pie-throwing area, paper plates, whipped cream, paper and cloth towels, moistened towelettes, tables, chairs, and a cash box with change.

Publicity and Promotion: Promote this event by displaying signs and giving out flyers at the sites of area businesses and organizations. The local media might publicize this fundraiser as part of their public-service announcements. The most effective publicity, however, will be at the site itself. Display posters near the ticket outlets and at the entrances to the event facility.

Time: This project can be planned within a day or so. Allow 2 weeks to gather the supplies and another week to find volunteer targets. Workers should be able to set up and take down the facility in less than 30 minutes.

Expenditures: Allocate $50 for promotional efforts. All supplies should be donated or loaned.

Personnel (Staff and Volunteers): A small group of volunteers (3-5) and a small staff (1-2) can successfully plan and implement the Pie Toss. Additional persons (6-10) serve as targets of the pie-throwing attempts. These volunteers should be well-known members of the community, such as city officials, teachers, and coaches.

RISK MANAGEMENT

The volunteers who serve as targets of the pie-throwing efforts should sign an agreement that absolves the organizers and the sponsoring group from liability except in the case of gross negligence. Only adult volunteers should be used as targets because minors are not allowed by law to waive their rights by exercising such agreements. Since almost all supplies and equipment needed for this fundraising project can be obtained on a donated or loan basis, there is no financial risk involved in this project.

PERMITS/LICENSES

None

HINTS

In all promotional efforts, highlight that this is a fundraising project, and specify how the profits from the Pie Toss will be used within the community. Dress the targets in a special T-shirt, blue jeans, and maybe a unique hat. Encourage these individuals to taunt potential throwers into buying (more) tickets. Publicly thank all of the volunteers whose efforts made this project a success. Donated awards can be given to those helpers whose efforts were especially noteworthy.

Personalized Athletic Footwear

POTENTIAL NET INCOME

$4,000

COMPLEXITY/DEGREE OF DIFFICULTY

Low

DESCRIPTION

This project involves selling personalized sneakers. The sneakers can be personalized with a variety of emblems, letters, numbers, and the like. One company that produces personalized gym shoes is D'BRIT Corporation, 6707 Old Dominion Drive, McLean, Virginia 22101 (800-666-7852). This company also has computer-generated stock emblems that may be selected to decorate the shoes. A percentage (15 percent to 50 percent) of the retail price, excluding taxes and shipping charges, is retained by the sponsoring organization. Money is collected when the orders are taken. The shoes are shipped directly to the customer from the manufacturer.

SCHEDULING

This fundraising project can be held at any time of the year. If the organizers plan to sell door-to-door, they should schedule this project to coincide with good weather.

RESOURCES

Facilities: None

Equipment and Supplies: The D'BRIT Corporation provides flyers, sales materials, and sample personalized shoes. The organization supplies posters.

Publicity and Promotion: Everyone is a potential customer. The primary advertising tactic is to widely distribute the handouts and to display the sample shoes. Advertising should appear in the local newspapers and advertising periodicals. Radio and television stations might mention this fundraiser as part of their public-service announcements. Local businesses and organizations can display posters, and some can accept orders. The manufacturer will provide additional sales suggestions. Advertising and order forms can be included in the organization's newsletters, sent through the school or employee mail system, and passed out at the next membership meeting or at an upcoming activity. Use the public-address system at other events to publicize this fundraising project. Emphasize the nonprofit nature of the sponsoring organization and explain how the money will be spent within the community.

Time: This project can be organized within 2 weeks. Allow 2 to 4 weeks to confirm the arrangements with the manufacturer. The selling window should be limited to 3 or 4 weeks. After the group's order has been sent to the manufacturer, the shoes will be shipped to the customers within 4 weeks.

Expenditures: This fundraiser can be implemented for less than $50 for publicity.

Personnel (Staff and Volunteers): A large group of dedicated volunteers (20-35) and a small staff (1-2) form the sales force. At least one adult is put in charge of record keeping, handling the money, and submitting the orders to the wholesaler.

RISK MANAGEMENT

There is no financial risk because the money for the shoes is collected up front. If youngsters are to be part of the sales force, they must be made aware of the safety aspects involved in going door-to-door. For example, children should not solicit at night or in strange neighborhoods without being accompanied by an adult. In some neighborhoods, youngsters should be accompanied by an adult at any time of the day.

PERMITS/LICENSES

If the shoes will be sold door-to-door, a peddler's permit may be needed. Check with the town clerk, local licensing bureau, or other municipal office.

HINTS

Choose a reputable company that will stand behind the product that your organization sells. The worst possible scenario is to be involved in selling shoddy merchandise within one's own community. To reap greater profits, conduct a training session for the salespersons. No hard-sell tactics are allowed.

Celebrity Auction

POTENTIAL NET INCOME

$4,000

COMPLEXITY/DEGREE OF DIFFICULTY

Low

DESCRIPTION

T-shirts, sport balls, baseball caps, scarves, and the like are mailed to celebrities throughout the country. Each item is accompanied by a personal request, on the sponsoring organization's stationery, that the celebrity autograph and/or decorate the item, then return it to the organization. These items are collected, stored, and then sold at a Celebrity Auction.

SCHEDULING

This auction can stand alone or be held in conjunction with another event.

RESOURCES

Facilities: A room in which the letters and items can be prepared to mail is needed. Storage of the returned items also will be necessary. The auction can take place in any large facility with room to accommodate 100 to 250 people.

Equipment and Supplies: The sponsoring organization provides the auction items, mailing containers, stationery, and postage. The use of a typewriter or word processing unit must be arranged. The auctioneer will need appropriate equipment, such as a portable microphone and record forms. Programs listing the celebrity items must be printed.

Publicity and Promotion: This fundraiser is concerned with two areas of promotion and publicity. First, the event must be promoted to the celebrities. The letters to the celebrities (or to their agents) should briefly relate the nonprofit nature of the organization, explain how the personalized items will be auctioned, and state how the money will be put to good use. This letter should be signed by two credible persons (perhaps the mayor of the community and the leader of the sponsoring organization). Accompanying each request is a prepaid, self-addressed envelope or box for the item to be returned to the organizers.

Second, the auction must be promoted to the public. Posters are displayed in stores, followed by timely mentions in the local media. Publicize some of the celebrity items to be auctioned.

Time: Planning for this fundraiser takes 1 to 2 weeks. Obtaining suitable items, then packaging and mailing them to the celebrities, can consume another 6 to 8 weeks. The auction can be completed within an hour or so.

Expenditures: The items to be sent to celebrities should be obtained free or at reduced cost. Ask local businesspersons to cover the mailing and packaging expenses. Even the printing of the program can be solicited for free or at low cost. Plan to spend $300 for whatever merchandise cannot be secured through donations and $200 for mailing containers and postage. Posters will run about $50. Many professional auctioneers will donate their services for nonprofit organizations.

Personnel (Staff and Volunteers): A professional auctioneer is a must. This adds sophistication to the event and thus increases the net profit. Several volunteers (10-15) and a small staff (1-2) help to obtain the auction items and then package and mail them to the celebrities. They promote the event and assist at the auction as spotters, cashiers, record keepers, and the like.

RISK MANAGEMENT

There is no financial risk associated with this event. The only danger is that insufficient items will be returned to support holding the auction. To increase the number of items returned by celebrities, the organizers must compose a convincing request. Make it a personal letter with a handwritten postscript at the bottom.

PERMITS/LICENSES

None

HINTS

Send a personal thank-you letter to each celebrity who participates in the fundraiser. Attempt to develop a relationship with these people by relating the success of the fundraising project and how the money was spent. Thank those who helped to obtain the personalized items from the celebrities. You might want to ask these people for assistance again.

Annual Sports Hall of Fame Luncheon

POTENTIAL NET INCOME

$3,500

COMPLEXITY/DEGREE OF DIFFICULTY

Moderate

DESCRIPTION

Former local athletic standouts (athletes, coaches, and administrators) are honored at a formal Hall of Fame luncheon. Any number of men and women may be inducted each year. Lunch is gratis for the master of ceremonies, the current inductees, and one guest per inductee; everyone else pays to attend. The profit comes from the sale of tickets, which are priced $20 over the cost of the meal and the use of the facility. With 200 paying guests, the net profit could easily reach $3,500.

SCHEDULING

If the sponsoring organization is a school, the luncheon can be scheduled just prior to the homecoming football game. The timing can be changed to make the event a dinner or breakfast affair.

RESOURCES

Facilities: The sponsoring organization must reserve a dining facility capable of seating at least 250 people. The room is arranged with a head table, tables seating ten persons each, and two buffet tables.

Equipment and Supplies: Donated plaques and framed certificates are presented to those inducted into the Hall of Fame. Duplicate plaques are permanently displayed in the athletic or recreation facility.

Publicity and Promotion: Formal invitations to the event are sent to family members and friends of the current and previous inductees, to athletic departments of every secondary school and college within the area, and to all athletic alumni. News releases, including photographs, are sent to the local media and to the media in the locale where the inductees currently reside.

Time: Planning this project will take at least 3 months. The luncheon will last no longer than 2 hours.

Expenditures: In addition to the cost of the meals, plan on spending $500 on printing invitations and programs and mailing the invitations. To gain greater profit, seek a corporate sponsor to underwrite all or a major portion of the expenses.

Personnel (Staff and Volunteers): A small number of volunteers and staff (5-7) serve as members of the selection committee. Other volunteers and staff members (10) mail invitations, order plaques and framed certificates, and sell tickets. A popular master of ceremonies must be found.

RISK MANAGEMENT

The major risk assumed in this fundraising event is the failure to attract a sufficient number of paying guests. Broadscale promotion of the luncheon and an attractive list of inductees should lure an adequate crowd for the first year. To ensure larger attendance in following years, invite and acknowledge all Hall of Fame members at each induction ceremony. This will entice these members and their families and friends to attend annually.

PERMITS/LICENSES

The food-service operators or owners of the restaurant are responsible for securing all food permits and licenses.

HINTS

Don't skimp on providing a formal atmosphere at the luncheon and securing a skilled master of ceremonies. These are the keys to making the event memorable.

The King and His Court Sport Exhibition

POTENTIAL NET INCOME

$4,000

COMPLEXITY/DEGREE OF DIFFICULTY

Moderate

DESCRIPTION

In this fundraiser, a semiprofessional or professional sport group puts on an exhibition or competes against a local team. One such touring group is the internationally acclaimed softball team, "The King and His Court." This four-man softball team can be contacted at P.O. Box 279, Ramona, California 92065-0279 (telephone: 619-390-8731). The profit is derived from the sale of concessions, souvenirs, and tickets (both in advance and at the door).

SCHEDULING

Friday evenings, Saturday afternoons and evenings, and Sunday afternoons are ideal for such an event. These are days when the entire family can spend time together and enjoy the fun.

RESOURCES

Facilities: An adequate sport facility that has a large seating capacity and adequate parking is required.

Equipment and Supplies: The sponsoring organization supplies the concession items, softballs, bats, bases, and so forth. If give-aways are to be part of the event, donated prizes are obtained. Posters and flyers are created to market the event. Don't forget rolls of tickets and a cash box with change.

Publicity and Promotion: This event should be marketed as an inexpensive family affair with opportunities to win prizes. Ticket sales depend on broadscale promotion of an attractive entertainment package. Trade tickets to the event for free advertising time on the radio and free space in newspapers. Display posters and flyers at local business sites, some of which can serve as ticket outlets. Highlight the opportunity to get autographs from the touring group. Conduct any number of promotional gimmicks, including giveaways at the event, to increase the attendance and the enjoyment of the crowd.

Time: The touring group may have to be scheduled 12 months in advance. Other planning for this event can take several weeks. Tickets are available 4 weeks prior to the game. The exhibition can be held within 2 hours; there could be several games on different days. For example, one game on Friday and two on Saturday, all for different audiences.

Expenditures: The payment to the touring group is customarily a flat rate of $2,500 per 9-inning game; this fee is paid out of the gate receipts. Plan to spend around $250 for advertising, tickets, and the wholesale cost of the merchandise and food to be sold at the event. Donated prizes are given away. Have $200 in change in the cash box at the door. Total expenses will be less than $3,000.

Personnel (Staff and Volunteers): A group of volunteers (30-35) working with a small staff (1-3) of the fundraising organization can effectively plan, market, and implement this project. Volunteers and staff can serve as members of the ground crew, ticket takers, umpires, the cleanup committee, and so forth. An opposing local team (perhaps representatives of the media) may agree to compete against the touring group.

RISK MANAGEMENT

There is a very real financial risk if insufficient tickets are sold to even cover expenses. There is no possibility of a rain date due to the tight schedule of the visiting team. Either establish a date by which the event can be cancelled (if insufficient advance tickets are sold) without financial obligation to the touring group, or secure financial backing through a business sponsor. In the latter arrangement, the sponsor agrees to pay the difference between the amount raised through sale of tickets and the expenses incurred, thus allowing the fundraising group to at least break even. This type of insurance is essential the first time this project is attempted. In terms of liability, the umbrella insurance policy of the sponsoring organization or of the site itself should be checked to ensure adequate coverage for this event.

PERMITS/LICENSES

Check local municipal offices about the need for a concession permit.

HINTS

The key to this fundraiser lies in selecting an entertaining touring group to compete against themselves or against the local all-star team. Check the phone directory of any large city to find agencies that book such groups.

Tailgate Parties

POTENTIAL NET INCOME
$4,000 per season

COMPLEXITY/DEGREE OF DIFFICULTY
Moderate

DESCRIPTION
The sponsoring organization plans tailgate parties to be held prior to various sporting contests or recreation activities throughout a calendar year. A specific area of an adjacent parking lot or a nearby grassy site is roped off for the exclusive use of the partyers. The "tailgaters" park their vehicles within this area. A nominal charge of $1, $2, or $3 per vehicle is charged, depending upon the popularity of the activity that follows the tailgate picnics and the availability of free parking nearby. In this designated area, people are encouraged to set up their portable grills, folding chairs and tables, coolers, and such in order to enjoy their picnics. For those who did not bring these items, ready-to-use grills are available for rent. Uncooked and cooked food, buns, condiments, and a variety of soft drinks are for sale. These gatherings provide opportunities for friends, fans, and boosters to congregate and express support for the sponsoring organization while having an enjoyable time. Following the tailgate activity, these people move on to the sporting or recreation event for more fun.

SCHEDULING
Each tailgate party begins 2 to 3 hours prior to a popular and highly anticipated sporting contest or recreation event.

RESOURCES
Facilities: Almost any outdoor area adjacent to the athletic or recreation site will suffice. A parking lot with an adjacent grassy area (for recreational activities) is ideal.

Equipment and Supplies: Gas and charcoal grills, fuel, signs, rope, safety cones, napkins, trash barrels, tables, chairs, a portable tent (in case of inclement weather), and a cash box are needed. A variety of food and drink to sell must also be on hand.

Publicity and Promotion: Announcements over the public-address system at other events of the sponsoring organization are very helpful. Mention in local newspapers and advertising periodicals can get the word out to the general public. Local merchants can display signs that promote the tailgate parties. Of course, the best promotional tactic of all is to ensure that those who attend the tailgate gathering have a truly great time.

Time: This fundraising project can be organized within a week. Publicity for each tailgate party should last at least 3 weeks. Plan to spend 2 to 3 hours setting up the site and another hour cleaning up the grounds afterward.

Expenditures: This fundraising project can be initiated for less than $300, including refreshments and promotional materials.

Personnel (Staff and Volunteers): Many volunteers (30-35) and a small staff (1-2) work on a rotating basis in the refreshment booth, give directions from the parking lot, and generally assist the partyers. Volunteers loan their grills for the day. Staff members, especially those whom the public would like to see and visit with, should make a point of attending the picnic.

RISK MANAGEMENT

To reduce liability exposure, organizers should assign adult volunteers to the parking lot to give directions and to curtail any potential rowdiness. All health rules must be strictly adhered to regarding the storage, preparation, and selling of food and drink. There is little financial risk because most unsold food and drink can be stored until the next tailgate party. Financial risk can be kept to a minimum by correctly anticipating the amount of food that must be defrosted.

PERMITS/LICENSES

A concession license may be necessary for the sale of food. If alcoholic beverages are to be sold, a separate permit may be needed. Check with the town clerk, the health department, or other municipal offices in your community.

HINTS

Some organizers sell beer at the tailgate parties, thus considerably boosting their net profit. Others sell apparel items if the crowd is large enough and the organization has a sufficient following. The key to a successful tailgate gathering is to provide opportunities for the participants to enjoy themselves by visiting with one another, eating out-of-doors, and engaging in fun recreational activities before they attend an athletic contest or recreation event. A well-organized tailgate party is not only enjoyable, it sets a positive tone for the activity that follows.

Perfect Gift for Secretaries Week

POTENTIAL NET INCOME
$4,500

COMPLEXITY/DEGREE OF DIFFICULTY
Moderate

DESCRIPTION
The "perfect gift" for secretaries consists of a basket filled with charming, useful, and fun gifts. Accompanying each basket is a handwritten card indicating who purchased the gift. If a person or a single business purchases five or more baskets, the sponsoring organization delivers the gift packages to the customer. All other purchasers pick up the baskets at a central location. Each gift basket sells for $20, of which about $18 is profit. If the sponsoring organization sells 250 baskets, the projected profit will be $4,500.

SCHEDULING
This fundraising activity is scheduled around National Secretaries Week, which is celebrated during the month of April. Purchasers pick up the baskets 3 days prior to the holiday.

RESOURCES
Facilities: A room where the gift items can be stored and the packages can be assembled and distributed is needed.

Equipment and Supplies: The sponsoring group must obtain the following items from area merchants for free: cards, baskets, tickets to museums and sporting events, desk plants, flower seeds, gift certificates for shopping and dining, discount car wash coupons, coupons for free cellular telephones, candy, coffee mugs, and stuffed animals. Flyers and posters are needed for publicity purposes.

Publicity and Promotion: Professional-looking flyers and posters are distributed throughout the area to businesses, schools, and corporations to publicize the gift baskets. The media frequently finds this type of fundraiser newsworthy under the category of community interest. Word of mouth is very effective. Emphasize the nonprofit nature of the organization and how the money raised will be put to good use within the community.

Time: The publicity and selling campaign should begin 4 to 5 weeks prior to the holiday to allow sufficient time for the orders to be received and the gift packages to be assembled. Plan on 5 to 6 weeks to collect the donated items. All baskets are distributed on a single day.

Expenditures: The sponsoring organization solicits all of the contents of the gift packages (including the baskets) on a free or greatly reduced basis. Plan to spend $500 in seed money, or $2 each for the 250 baskets sold; postage; paid advertising; and the cost of creating signs and posters. However, some of these items and services, too, can be obtained on a donated basis.

Personnel (Staff and Volunteers): A large, well-trained group of volunteers (35-50) supporting a small staff (2-4) can make this project a huge success. They take orders for the baskets, solicit free gift items from merchants, organize the gifts, and assemble the baskets. A volunteer skilled in calligraphy is needed to write the cards accompanying each gift. If any baskets are to be delivered, volunteers with vehicles will be needed to fulfill this duty.

RISK MANAGEMENT

There are no risks involved in this activity, either in terms of finances or liability. The gift baskets are created after the orders are received. The sponsors *must* secure the gift items prior to advertising that these gifts will be included in the baskets.

PERMITS/LICENSES

None

HINTS

People will buy the gift baskets because of the quality and quantity of the gift items and because of the nonprofit status of the sponsoring group. Public thanks should be given to those companies and individuals who contributed the contents of the gift baskets. The sponsoring organization might want to put a limit on the number of baskets (perhaps 300) that they will attempt to sell. Doing so provides a specific goal and helps to motivate the sales force. This also simplifies the solicitation of free gift items because the donors will know exactly how many they will be contributing to the fundraising activity.

Limousine Scavenger Hunt

POTENTIAL NET INCOME
$4,400

COMPLEXITY/DEGREE OF DIFFICULTY
Low

DESCRIPTION
Teams comprised of six members compete against one another to locate and retrieve more than 100 diverse items, all of which can be located within the city limits. The scavenger list contains more items than possibly could be obtained by the contestants within the time allowed. The list includes zany, hard-to-find items, such as a ticket stub from a local athletic event, an old license plate, a signature from a local television personality, a napkin from a specific restaurant, or a tie with an animal on it. Each team travels in a limousine driven by a volunteer. Various corporate sponsors defray the expenses associated with this fundraiser, including the cost of the limousines, prizes, and publicity. Each team pays an entry fee of $300. Teams may be sponsored by businesses and organizations, or the team members can chip in $50 apiece to be a part of this fun-filled afternoon. This fundraiser can be scheduled as an annual event. If so, as many as 15 teams can be expected to take part in the initial year's hunt, with more teams competing in subsequent years for top honors as the best scavengers in the community. All contestants receive a hat and a T-shirt to commemorate their involvement in the Limousine Scavenger Hunt.

SCHEDULING
The scavenger hunt is scheduled for a Saturday or Sunday afternoon. The event can take place at any time of the year.

RESOURCES

Facilities: The sponsoring organization must secure a site at which to count the scavengers' collected items and to award donated prizes to the winning team members.

Equipment and Supplies: Posters, displays, flyers, and sheets listing the items to be hunted are necessary. Donated imprinted baseball hats and screened T-shirts are needed for all of the contestants. The prizes also are donated and can include meals at various restaurants, car washes, and trips to professional athletic events. Loaned limousines and volunteer drivers transport the competing teams on their hunts.

Publicity and Promotion: Person-to-person contact with area businesses and organizations, as well as with individuals, is essential for obtaining a sufficient number of teams for the scavenger hunt. Publicity involves announcements in area newspapers and advertising periodicals. Local radio and television stations might mention this fundraiser as part of their public-service announcements. Businesses can display posters promoting the upcoming event. Public-address announcements concerning the scavenger hunt can be made at other community sport and recreation activities. Following the conclusion of the scavenger hunt, photograph the winning team and then send pictures with news releases to the area newspapers for possible feature stories. These photos also can be used for the following year's publicity for the event. In all promotional efforts, highlight the fact that this project is organized by a local, nonprofit organization and that the net profits will go for a specific worthy cause within the community.

Time: The hunt itself can be planned within a week. Allow 3 to 4 weeks to line up the prizes, sponsors, competing team members, and volunteers to help with the event. The publicity prior to the scavenger hunt lasts 3 to 4 weeks. All entry forms and fees should be received at least 2 weeks prior to the date of the event. The scavenger hunt lasts 3 hours.

Expenditures: This fundraising project can be initiated for less than $100, to be spent primarily for publicity purposes.

Personnel (Staff and Volunteers): Several volunteers (10-15) and a small staff (2-4) are needed to plan and implement this fundraiser. Additional helpers (15) solicit sponsors for the event and drive the limousines.

RISK MANAGEMENT

There is no financial risk because the scavenger hunt is not initiated until the entry fees have been received. Check to ensure that the insurance policy covering the limousines and their drivers is in force and covers this type of activity.

PERMITS/LICENSES

Each of the drivers must have a current driver's license for a commercial vehicle.

HINTS

If sufficient limousines are not available, teams could be transported by vans donated by individuals and businesses. If the contestants enjoy themselves, there will be increased participation in subsequent years.

Coat Check Service

POTENTIAL NET INCOME

$4,400 per season

COMPLEXITY/DEGREE OF DIFFICULTY

Low

DESCRIPTION

A coat and hat check service is set up for each athletic contest or recreation activity. The coat check operation is staffed by volunteers, and a minimal amount is charged to provide this service of security and convenience for the patrons present at the event. Fifty-cents per person is reasonable, but charge whatever is customary in your area. The average gross income for each event is $75. If the sponsoring organization is involved in 60 events during the year when the coat check service is appropriate, the group would expect a net profit of $4,400 annually.

SCHEDULING

This fundraiser is suitable for any indoor activity where the patrons will be arriving in coats and hats.

RESOURCES

Facilities: A room or cordoned-off area is needed where the coats and hats can be safely deposited until the owners return to claim them. The location must be in close proximity to the door where the patrons will be entering and exiting the building. A room must be available to store unclaimed articles (for a minimum of 6 months).

Equipment and Supplies: Paired, consecutively numbered, plastic tabs or two-part tickets are essential to identify the ownership of the checked items. The organization borrows hangers and portable metal coatracks or stands. Signs are created with donated materials.

Publicity and Promotion: At the site where the coat check is set up, there should be highly visible signs promoting the service. Publicize on the signs that this is a fundraising effort and state how the profits will be put to use by the nonprofit sponsoring organization. Use the public-address system to announce to the crowd the availability of the coat check operation.

Time: This fundraising project can be planned in 1 or 2 days. The coat check operation should be open for business at least 1 hour prior to the start of the event. Volunteers stay until the last item is claimed. This fundraising effort can be repeated throughout the year, at least as long as the weather is cold or wet.

Expenditures: The only cost for this project will be for 200 consecutively numbered paired plastic tabs, which can be used repeatedly. Allot 50 cents for each tab, and buy 10 percent more than you anticipate using on any given date because a number of the tabs will be lost during the year.

Personnel (Staff and Volunteers): Plan to staff the coat check operation with 2 to 3 volunteers at a time, with each working a 2-hour shift. For example, if an event lasts from 6 P.M. until 10 P.M., the coat check operation will be staffed from 5 P.M. until approximately 11:00 P.M.; during these 6 hours, 6 to 9 volunteers should serve the patrons.

RISK MANAGEMENT

The financial exposure in terms of economic loss is minimal in the sense that there are no significant expenses involved in setting up the coat check operation. However, there is the potential for damages claimed for damaged or lost items. Thus, the organizers must prominently display a sign that reads "Operators Are Not Responsible for Loss or Damage to Items Checked." This notice helps to protect the organization against damage claims. Check with the insurance agencies that provide coverage for the site and for the sponsoring organization to learn what other steps can be taken to reduce liability. If there are any items left unclaimed after an event, these must be stored in a secure place until claimed by the owners. Unclaimed items should be kept for at least 6 months (or whatever the law requires in your area) and then donated to a charitable organization.

PERMITS/LICENSES

None

HINTS

This is an easy fundraising project that can generate sizeable profits with minimal risk and little financial investment. The organizers can garner significant positive public relations if they provide adequate and speedy service to the patrons attending the event. To bring in additional profit, place a glass jar at the coat check site, and insert several dollar bills in the jar before opening for business. Provide a sign stating that cash contributions to the nonprofit organization would be greatly appreciated. Highlight the purpose for which these donations will be used.

Home Run
Fundraising Program

POTENTIAL NET INCOME
$4,500

COMPLEXITY/DEGREE OF DIFFICULTY
Low

DESCRIPTION
The sponsoring organization solicits pledges from donors based on the number of home runs a softball team or baseball team hits during a season. Pledges can range from $1 to $5 per home run. In addition to the pledges contributed to the team, each of the donors receives a weekly team newsletter and a booster's ball cap.

SCHEDULING
The solicitation of pledges should take place one month prior to the opening of spring training for the professional baseball teams. This timing takes advantage of the attention and enthusiasm being focused on the sports of baseball and softball.

RESOURCES
Facilities: None

Equipment and Supplies: The organization orders professionally created pledge cards. Signs and flyers are needed to describe the fundraiser and to explain how the money will be used. A newsletter is provided, and imprinted hats are given to the donors. Two giant thermometers are constructed.

Publicity and Promotion: Display posters and flyers in stores, and distribute news releases to the local media. Solicit on a personal basis, using visits, telephone calls, and the mail. At each home game, promote the Home Run Fundraising Program. Emphasize how the money will be spent. To motivate the community and the fans in attendance, display a giant thermometer in a highly visible location near the ball field and another outside the sponsoring organization's facility. The sign should display the current amount raised.

Time: The solicitation of pledges before the season begins can be completed within 4 weeks. Additional pledges can be accepted at any time during the season. Never refuse money.

Expenditures: Plan to spend $200 for initial advertising and promotional activities, including the printing of posters, flyers, pledge cards, and newsletters. Many of these might be provided on a donated basis. The booster's caps also should be donated.

Personnel (Staff and Volunteers): Staff members, athletes, and many volunteers (40-50) form an effective sales force to solicit the pledges prior to the start of the season and then to collect the money following the season's finale. Staff members or other adults must be given responsibility for handling the money and be held accountable.

RISK MANAGEMENT

This project involves no financial risks or liability exposure. To prevent surprises and criticism against the organization, the solicitors should relate to potential contributors the average number of home runs hit by the team during the previous three seasons. An alternate method of keeping the contributions predictable is to establish a cap on the amount of each donation.

PERMITS/LICENSES

Some communities require a peddler's permit to solicit door-to-door.

HINTS

After the season has ended, the promoters might want to have a picnic for the coaches, players, parents, and all the contributors to the Home Run Fundraising Program. One goal of this gathering is to acknowledge those individuals and businesses who contributed to the sport program through their pledges. Thus, if the promoters wish to repeat this fundraiser, they can approach previous donors who have had a positive experience with their involvement.

Santa's Workshop

POTENTIAL NET INCOME
$4,000

COMPLEXITY/DEGREE OF DIFFICULTY
High

DESCRIPTION
Santa's Workshop is created by making alterations to a vacant building; by erecting a complete, temporary structure; or by renovating part of the sponsoring organization's facility. The area is converted into a beautiful Christmas wonderland that provides an enjoyable holiday experience for youngsters and adults alike. Children can have their pictures taken with Santa, visit with elves, and marvel at the exquisite scenes involving an extensive array of lights, music, and activities. Profits are generated from the sale of tickets, food, and drink.

The admission charge is $3 per child, and parents attend free. Adults attending without children are charged $3. If 1,500 paying customers tour the facility during the 4 weeks that it is open, the gross profit will be $4,500. Ticket prices may vary in light of what the market will bear and the type of Santa's Workshop created.

SCHEDULING
Santa's Workshop is held throughout the month of December.

RESOURCES
Facilities: The sponsoring organization must secure a suitable building or structure that can easily be converted into a Christmas environment. The site must be easily accessible and near a high volume of vehicular traffic. Ample and safe parking is required.

Equipment and Supplies: A sound system, tapes or compact discs, signs, a variety of Christmas decorations, decorated trees, costumes for Santa and the elves, lighting, and so forth are necessary to create a realistic experience. One or more Polaroid cameras plus an adequate supply of film is needed. Safety equipment (emergency lighting and fire extinguishers) is required. All items should be obtained gratis or on a loan basis.

Publicity and Promotion: The publicity consists of promotional activities and announcements displayed in area businesses. Outdoor signs adjacent to the facility should be erected as early as Thanksgiving. The media might provide free mention of this fundraiser due to the nonprofit nature of the effort. Notices and flyers should be sent to all local schools, day care centers, and churches. Individual person-to-person contacts are invaluable in helping to spread the word and in motivating greater participation. Always emphasize the fun aspect of the event in conjunction with how the money will be used.

Time: Planning for this fundraiser can be completed within 3 weeks. Allot 2 weeks to get commitments from volunteers and to confirm the use of the facility and 5 weeks to secure donated items or items on loan. Allow 3 weeks to complete the physical transformation of the site. Cleanup will take 1 week.

Expenditures: Donated items and services can significantly reduce the cost of transforming the facility into Santa's Workshop, then back again. Costs include signs, banners, and other promotional items. Costumes must be made for Santa and the elves. Film for the Polaroid camera is necessary. Allocate $500 for materials and services that cannot be obtained on a donated or loan basis.

Personnel (Staff and Volunteers): A large cadre (35-50) of staff and volunteers, including skilled craftspeople (e.g., carpenters, electricians), is needed to create the physical changes in Santa's Workshop. Volunteers staff the site, sell tickets, and serve as Santa and the elves.

RISK MANAGEMENT

Check to ascertain that the site's blanket insurance policy provides sufficient liability coverage. Whenever a large number of people are expected to move through a structure that has been altered significantly from its original state, accident prevention and liability exposure are always a concern.

PERMITS/LICENSES

Check with the local building inspector to find out if permits are needed to make significant alterations to the facility. Call the local department of health to ask if a concession stand requires a permit.

Special attention must be paid to electrical and other safety codes in order to ensure a safe environment for all.

HINTS

The net profit depends to a great extent upon the amount of money that can be saved by obtaining donated services and goods. Many items might be borrowed. If outside activities are to be added to this fundraiser, consider sleigh rides (tractors and wagons) and any number of games, contests, and sing-alongs.

Gift Wrapping

POTENTIAL NET INCOME

$4,800

COMPLEXITY/DEGREE OF DIFFICULTY

Moderate

DESCRIPTION

During the Christmas season, volunteers of the sponsoring organization set up tables at one or more locations within the community and charge modest fees for quality gift wrapping. Prices for various package sizes should be prominently displayed at the site(s), along with samples of the gift wrapping. If, on an average, a $2 profit is made on each item wrapped, a well-organized and dedicated group of volunteers can easily net $4,800 during the holidays.

SCHEDULING

The gift-wrapping tables can open for business during the evenings and throughout the weekends during the early weeks of December. During the last week before Christmas, gift wrapping can be available from 11 A.M. until closing time each day of the week.

RESOURCES

Facilities: The sponsoring organization obtains permission to set up gift-wrapping tables inside shopping centers and malls. The gift-wrapping service also can be set up at a central location within the community, such as a school, recreation center, or even a community hospital. High traffic and adequate parking near each site are necessary. Tables also may be set up for business preceding and following various sporting events and recreation activities. This type of site is especially effective if sport merchandise is sold there.

Equipment and Supplies: The organization must obtain tables, chairs, signs, wrapping paper, boxes, ribbons, bows, string, tape, gift tags, cash boxes, and receipt books. A portable booth may be erected in malls and shopping centers.

Publicity and Promotion: Advertisements promoting the gift-wrapping service should be placed in area newspapers and advertising periodicals. Local radio and television stations might provide free public-service announcements. Businesses and organizations can display posters promoting the service. Emphasize that this is a fundraising project sponsored by a worthy, nonprofit organization. State how the profits from this project will be spent.

Time: This fundraising project can be planned and organized within a week. The first tasks are to identify appropriate sites and to obtain permission to set up the gift-wrapping operations. Allow 5 weeks to obtain the gift wrapping and assorted supplies. Advertising efforts are ongoing from mid-November through Christmas.

Expenditures: Allocate $200 in seed money. The gift-wrapping materials can be donated or bought at a discount. The tables and chairs should be borrowed, and the posters can be obtained free or at reduced cost. If a portable booth is to be used, obtain donated materials and labor.

Personnel (Staff and Volunteers): The key to the success of this project is having sufficient helpers who are skilled in wrapping gifts. Don't expect volunteers to become experts in wrapping without training and practice. The organizers should hold one or more training sessions during which volunteers are taught the art of gift wrapping. The number of necessary volunteers will depend on the number of sites set up and the hours that each gift wrapping site is open to the public. This fundraising project can be time intensive; plan to involve 35 to 55 volunteers. If the organizers plan to have a booth built, they will need the donated services of carpenters.

RISK MANAGEMENT

The financial risks, although minimal, revolve around the costs (if any) of the gift-wrapping supplies. To prevent the situation in which the organization is stuck with a large supply of unused gift wrapping and associated material, there should be an agreement that all unopened boxes of supplies may be returned for a full refund. There is no liability exposure involved in this fundraising project as long as permission is obtained prior to setting up the gift-wrapping tables.

PERMITS/LICENSES

If the gift-wrapping tables are to be set up in a store or mall, be sure to receive written permission to do so. Some stores have their own gift-wrapping service and would not want competition at their own sites. Some managers might be hesitant to grant permission because they may not want to risk having their customers being dissatisfied with the gift wrapping done by the nonprofit organization, fearing this might reflect negatively upon their facility. To counteract this objection, provide samples of the gift wrapping that your group will provide.

HINTS

Gift-wrapping is a natural annual fundraising project—one that can result in significant financial profits for the organization and good will from the community. If this is to be an annual event, the organization can get a jump on the following year's gift-wrapping project by securing the names, addresses, and phone numbers of the customers who took advantage of the service during the initial year. This easily can be accomplished by conducting a raffle for one or more donated gifts to be given away after Christmas. In order to enter the raffle, the customers must fill out entry slips that require their names, addresses, and phone numbers, and then deposit them in a large fishbowl. Early the following November, the organizers mail a postcard or letter to these people stating that the holiday gift-wrapping service again will take place during December. This reminder includes the location of the various gift-wrapping sites for the upcoming season.

Win-a-Car
Basketball Toss

POTENTIAL NET INCOME

$4,900

COMPLEXITY/DEGREE OF DIFFICULTY

Moderate

DESCRIPTION

Tickets are sold for $1 each at every athletic contest held by a sport organization for the chance to shoot a basketball from three-quarter or full court during the final basketball game of the season. At the final game, all of the tickets are placed in a large container, and one lucky ticket is pulled. The person with the winning ticket wins the opportunity to make the super-long shot. If successful, the shooter wins a new car. Prior to the drawing, the sponsoring organization secures an insurance policy against the possibility that the attempt will be successful and the car must be given away.

SCHEDULING

The winning attempt is to take place at halftime of the last regularly scheduled basketball game of the season.

RESOURCES

Facilities: A basketball court is needed.

Equipment and Supplies: A table and chairs are set up at each athletic contest at which tickets will be sold. A large bowl or revolving drum is used to contain the drawing tickets. Two-part tickets must be obtained; one part of each ticket is retained by the purchaser, and the matching stub goes into the bowl or drum for the eventual drawing. Of course, a basketball is needed.

Publicity and Promotion: Signs are displayed at all athletic contests and at various businesses and organizations within the community. The news media should publicize this event as part of their public-service announcements. Display the car that may be won (or enlarged photographs of the vehicle) at the various athletic events. Pull out all the stops in promoting this fundraiser at the last home basketball game, during which the actual attempt will be made. For several weeks prior to that date, news releases should be sent to the media hyping the upcoming event.

On the big night, two exciting events take place. First, there is the drawing of the ticket that gives the holder the right to attempt the long shot. Second, there is the excitement of the shot itself and the possibility of the car being won. Have both a video photographer and a still photographer on hand for the attempt. This photography will be especially important for news releases if the shot is successful. Even if the shot is unsuccessful, the excitement should be recorded for prosperity and used to promote a possible repeat contest.

Time: Although the winning basketball toss is conducted at the season's last home game of the sponsoring organization, tickets are sold at every athletic contest for all sports throughout the entire year. Planning for this event and lining up a suitable insurance policy in case the three-quarter or full-court shot is successful can take 2 to 3 weeks. The winning attempt and the related activities takes less than 5 minutes.

Expenditures: Plan to spend up to $750 on the insurance coverage, tickets, promotional efforts, and the drum or bowl from which the winning ticket is to be drawn.

Personnel (Staff and Volunteers): A few volunteers (3) and a small staff (2) can plan and implement this fundraiser. Many more volunteers (35-50) are needed on a rotating basis to sell the tickets at each of the athletic events throughout the year. The staff and a few of the adult volunteers should supervise the shot attempt.

RISK MANAGEMENT

The risk involved in this fundraiser is that the shot will be made and the car won. Therefore, the sponsoring organization must secure an insurance policy against this possibility. Videotaping the shot attempt and having adult supervisors and a representative of the insurance company witness the shot will prevent any misunderstandings in terms of the rules governing the contest. There are no other financial or liability risks in this fundraiser.

PERMITS/LICENSES

Since this is a form of gambling, you may be required to secure a game-of-chance permit or gambling license in your area. Check with the local municipal offices or police agency.

HINTS

Strict rules must be enforced in terms of how far back from the basket the shooter must stand. Some insurers may insist that the attempt take place at the three-quarter mark, while others may require a full-court attempt. Some insurance policies may stipulate that basketball players are excluded from being contestants. One company that is involved in special sport promotions and provides bonded guarantees and funding of contingent prizes for halftime events is SCA Promotions, 8300 Douglas Avenue, Dallas, Texas 75225 (800-527-5409).

A possible alternative to buying insurance is to find a car dealership willing to donate the car, if won, in exchange for the publicity involved.

PART III

FUNDRAISERS GENERATING FROM $5,000 TO $10,000

38

Turkey Raffle

POTENTIAL NET INCOME

$5,500

COMPLEXITY/DEGREE OF DIFFICULTY

Low

DESCRIPTION

The Turkey Raffle provides an affordable, fun-filled afternoon or evening of activities for the whole family. Raffle tickets for numerous frozen turkeys (40-75) are sold for 50 cents each, or whatever the market will bear. Expect a crowd of 500 or larger and raffle ticket sales of 8,000 or more. Some organizers provide limited free refreshments; Others provide a concession stand that will bring in additional profit. An admission charge of $1 per person or per family may be charged. In addition to raffling frozen turkeys, the sponsoring organization can give away numerous door prizes, such as portable televisions, radios, and tickets to professional athletic events.

SCHEDULING

The raffle is held on the weekend before Thanksgiving.

RESOURCES

Facilities: A hall or auditorium capable of accommodating 500 to 750 people is necessary. A school gymnasium or recreation center may be suitable. Adequate parking is a must.

Equipment and Supplies: Tables, chairs, a public-address system, frozen turkeys, door prizes, a drum or huge glass bowl, tickets, flyers, and posters are necessary.

Publicity and Promotion: Extensive word-of-mouth publicity is vital for this fundraiser. Area businesses and organizations can display posters advertising the upcoming Turkey Raffle and festivities. Local television and radio stations might publicize this fundraiser as part of their public-service announcements. Area newspapers and advertising periodicals should be approached about including free coverage both before and after the Turkey Raffle. A picture of children holding turkeys that they won makes a great photo for the town paper. Publicize that this is a fundraising project by a local, nonprofit organization, and highlight how the profits are going to be used in the community.

Time: The Turkey Raffle can be organized within a few days. Allow several weeks to make firm arrangements with the turkey wholesaler. Reserve the use of the site as early as possible. Allow 4 to 5 weeks for publicity and promotional efforts. The Turkey Raffle festivities can last between 3 and 5 hours, depending upon what activities are planned. Setting up the facility will take 2 to 3 hours, and cleanup efforts will consume an hour or more.

Expenditures: Allocate $150 for promotional supplies. The turkeys should be donated. If they must be purchased, be sure to receive a steep discount from the wholesaler.

Personnel (Staff and Volunteers): Many volunteers (25) and a small staff (1-2) are needed to plan and promote the Turkey Raffle. These same helpers staff the event and handle the various activities and the raffle itself. A colorful master of ceremonies is a great asset in moving the raffle drawing along at a brisk pace and in getting the crowd involved in the excitement of the drawings. Volunteers and staff members who are particularly influential should find people to donate door prizes to be raffled.

RISK MANAGEMENT

At the initial Turkey Raffle, there is a risk that insufficient people will attend. To prevent financial disaster, the organizers must extensively and effectively promote this fundraiser. To reduce liability exposure, obtain the frozen turkeys only from a reputable wholesaler.

PERMITS/LICENSES

Since the Turkey Raffle is a form of gambling, check with the local town clerk or police authority to determine whether any state or local permits or licenses are required.

HINTS

The atmosphere at the Turkey Raffle should be charged with energy and anticipation. The affair should be a large party where all of the participants' families and friends are present. Both children and adults will return year after year if they have a fun time. If held annually, supporting the Turkey Raffle may become almost as strong a tradition as celebrating Thanksgiving itself. Some organizations provide games of chance for the adults, as well as recreational games and contests for the youngsters. Some turkey raffles are structured so that the winners are selected by having their tickets picked individually out of a bowl or large box. Other raffles use a spinning wheel to identify the lucky winners. Some events even piggyback a dinner along with the Turkey Raffle.

Selling Christmas Trees

POTENTIAL NET INCOME

$5,900

COMPLEXITY/DEGREE OF DIFFICULTY

Moderate

DESCRIPTION

The sponsoring organization sells Christmas trees and makes arrangements with the customers to pick up the trees at a central location during a 3- to 4-day period a few weeks before Christmas. Four hundred trees sold at a profit of $15 each would generate $6,000 in profit, minus selling and advertising costs.

SCHEDULING

It is necessary to make prior arrangements with a reputable Christmas tree farm to purchase a number of trees for specific prices, depending upon the height of each tree. Once the sponsoring organization has the customers' orders and payment in hand, the group can confirm the order of a specific number of trees of varying heights.

RESOURCES

Facilities: A site must be secured where the trees can be stored and distributed once they arrive from the tree farm.

Equipment and Supplies: Order forms and record books are needed, as are lights and signs for the site where the trees will be distributed.

Publicity and Promotion: Distribute signs several weeks prior to the time at which advance orders will be taken. If this fundraising activity is to become an annual event, the initial effort will establish acceptance, and the marketing and selling of the trees in subsequent seasons will be expedited.

Time: The selling window should be 2 to 3 weeks. The time period for the distribution of the trees can be as few as 3 or 4 days during specific hours.

Expenditures: No money is paid to the tree farm until after the selling period, when the order for the trees is confirmed. Forty percent of the cost may then be put down as a deposit, with the rest to be paid upon delivery of the trees. By the time that the order is placed, all the money will have been received from those who had ordered the Christmas trees. The cost of preprinted order forms and signs should be less than $100, especially if some items are donated or bought at reduced prices.

Personnel (Staff and Volunteers): Numerous staff members and volunteers (30-50) should be involved in marketing and selling the trees. Helpers are needed to keep records of the orders and money. People also are needed to handle the trees and provide security after they have been delivered to the distribution site.

RISK MANAGEMENT

The importance of dealing with a reputable tree farm cannot be overemphasized. If possible, personally visit the owner(s) and state the worthy nature of the organization's fundraising effort. Indicate that this activity could become an annual event. Provide adequate lighting at the distribution site to reduce the risk of accidents.

PERMITS/LICENSES

Contact the town clerk or the municipal offices to find out whether any local ordinances cover this type of fundraising activity.

HINTS

Negotiate the cost of the trees so that transportation costs are included. Ascertain that the trees are guaranteed to be delivered on a specific date and at a specific location determined by the purchasing organization. All orders must be accompanied with cash or checks so that the sponsoring group will have all of the money prior to confirming the final order with the tree farm. Checks from those placing orders should be cashed prior to placing the final order.

Candy Bar Sale

POTENTIAL NET INCOME

$6,000

COMPLEXITY/DEGREE OF DIFFICULTY

Low

DESCRIPTION

Candy bars purchased from a wholesaler are sold by both adults and youngsters. The candy bars cost 50 cents each and are sold for $1. The wrapping on each bar shows the logo and name of the sponsoring organization. Donated prizes are given to top salespersons in the different age categories.

SCHEDULING

This simple project can be initiated at any time of the year. However, if the candy is to be sold door-to-door, this fundraiser should be implemented during nice weather.

RESOURCES

Facilities: The organization selects a site where the candy can be shipped from the wholesaler.

Equipment and Supplies: Signs, flyers, candy bars, donated prizes, and receipt books are necessary. The volunteers must carry sufficient change when they canvass individual homes for candy sales.

Publicity and Promotion: Announcements of the upcoming candy sale should be included in local papers and advertising periodicals. Area businesses can display signs promoting the sale. Announcements should be made over the public-address system at area athletic contests or recreation activities. The candy bars themselves will be the primary impetus for the purchase of the candy. In all of the promotional efforts, highlight how the profits will be used.

Time: Allow 2 to 3 weeks for the delivery of the merchandise from the wholesaler. Keep the selling window to a maximum of 2 weeks. Dragging out the candy sale becomes a boring and burdensome experience for all concerned.

Expenditures: Allocate $100 for posters and paid advertisements. Prizes are donated from area businesses. The candy bars are paid for out of the profits, usually after the selling period is over.

Personnel (Staff and Volunteers): A large number of volunteers (50-75) are needed to market the candy bars throughout the community. Youngsters can canvass local neighborhoods; adults can sell the candy to their coworkers, friends, and neighbors. Volunteers also can sell the candy at sport contests or recreation activities sponsored by the selling organization. For the sake of security, have a few (2-3) adults handle all of the merchandise orders, maintain records, and deposit the money collected.

RISK MANAGEMENT

Purchase the candy bars in bulk from a reputable wholesaler only. The sponsoring organization would not want to sell candy that is stale or otherwise of poor quality. Most wholesalers will agree not to bill the nonprofit organization for the candy bars until 30 to 60 days following delivery. This allows the soliciting group to sell the candy bars and then pay for them from the profits of the campaign. As long as unsold candy (in unopened boxes) can be returned to the wholesaler, the financial risk is minimal. Have a training session to educate and motivate the youngsters and adults who will be involved in selling the candy. Youngsters should be warned against selling in strange neighborhoods or at night without adult supervision. No hard-sell tactics should be used by the sales personnel.

PERMITS/LICENSES

If the candy bars are to be sold door-to-door, the organization may need to obtain a peddler's permit. Check with the town clerk or the municipal bureau of licenses in your community.

HINTS

Since some wholesalers allow the return of unsold candy if the boxes have not been opened, don't get in a hurry and open every box unless you are sure that you can sell all the merchandise. If there is candy left over after the selling window is completed, give these unsold bars to the top salespersons and have them attempt to sell them over a single weekend. There are numerous candy wholesalers that will provide a wide selection of candy for fundraisers. One such company is Niagara Candy Company, 3500 Genesee, Buffalo, New York 14225 (716-634-4545).

Piggyback Fundraising Solicitation Letter

POTENTIAL NET INCOME
$6,000

COMPLEXITY/DEGREE OF DIFFICULTY
Low

DESCRIPTION
A solicitation letter or card is mailed on behalf of a nonprofit organization by inserting (piggyback style) the promotional piece inside another organization's regular mass mailing within the community. Any company or organization that periodically sends such a mailing is a prime candidate to approach for this fundraising effort. The solicitation card or letter promotes the sport or recreation organization, justifies donations, and requests that contributions be mailed directly to the organizing group's headquarters. Or, if the company making the mailing will agree, the contributions may be sent directly to that company, whose personnel will collect, tally, and deposit the contributions on behalf of the sponsoring organization.

SCHEDULING
This type of fundraising effort can take place at any time of the year other than around major holidays.

RESOURCES
Facilities: A room is needed in which to create the insert.

Equipment and Supplies: A personal computer, word processing software, and high-quality color card stock or bond paper is used to create a professional-looking insert.

Publicity and Promotion: There is no need for advance publicity and promotional activities. However, your efforts will be to no avail if the solicitation piece fails to motivate people to contribute to a worthy cause. The solicitation must publicize the worthiness of the nonprofit organization and highlight an obvious need or project to which the donations will be allocated. Remember that brevity coupled with clarity are twin virtues in terms of any printed solicitation effort.

Time: Allow several months to plan this fundraiser and to arrange the cooperation of a company that engages in mass mailings. Plan to spend at least 1 week creating and printing the inserts. The solicitation cards or letters should be ready to mail at least 3 weeks prior to the date of the mass mailing.

Expenditures: Allocate $200 to create and print the solicitation piece. The use of the computer and software should be donated. There would be no cost involved at all if the company making the mailing (or other organizations or individuals) would pay for the solicitation pieces. Organizers should never hesitate to ask for such assistance.

Personnel (Staff and Volunteers): Minimal personnel (5) are necessary. Assistance in designing and printing the solicitation piece may be needed if the company making the mass mailing will not perform these tasks. Influential persons are called upon to convince a company to allow the sport or recreation organization to include an insert in its regular mass mailing. Companies agree to help because (1) they believe the money will be used for a good purpose, and (2) they respond to the requests of influential persons. Thus, the value of having such individuals make the pleas for help cannot be overstated.

RISK MANAGEMENT

The risks inherent in this fundraiser are minimal. There are no significant financial risks or liability exposure. Of course, care must be taken to ensure that the solicitation insert fits in the mailing envelope, that the format and contents of the mailing are appropriately designed, and that the message is both convincing in the solicitation of funds and compatible with the image of the company doing the mailing.

PERMITS/LICENSES

None

HINTS

Some examples of companies that might be approached are banks, telephone companies, utility (water, gas, electric) companies, major department stores, and the like. Even the free area weekly newspapers can be approached to insert a solicitation piece that promotes a good cause. The concept of a mass mailing insert also can be used to promote a sport or recreation organization's future fundraising project or other special event—either in addition to or in place of the specific fundraising solicitation appeal outlined above.

Beach Towels for Sale

POTENTIAL NET INCOME

$6,000

COMPLEXITY/DEGREE OF DIFFICULTY

Low

DESCRIPTION

Beach towels with a beautiful two-color insignia or mascot design representing the sponsoring organization are sold at a price that provides a $10 net profit each. Companies that specialize in producing such towels can be located through the yellow pages of the telephone directory, at the library, or by contacting the athletic offices of nearby colleges or universities. Sales may be made on a take-order (advance order) basis or point-of-sale

("show and sell") basis. In the first instance, orders are taken from customers, then the towels are ordered from the wholesaler. The towels are later delivered to each purchaser and the money is collected. The point-of-sale method requires first obtaining the towels, then selling them to the customers.

SCHEDULING

This fundraiser can be initiated at any time of the year. However, the late winter and early spring months are ideal selling periods for this product because the summer months will be approaching soon.

RESOURCES

Facilities: The organization must locate a site where the towels can be stored until they are sold.

Equipment and Supplies: A receipt book, record book, and posters are required. Prizes and awards to be given to top salespersons should be donated by area businesses.

Publicity and Promotion: Making the community aware of the upcoming fundraising effort paves the way toward better sales. Publicity in the area news media and advertising periodicals is essential. Place posters publicizing the availability of the towels at the sites of businesses and organizations. Some stores might bolster sales by taking some towels on consignment. It is important to note that person-to-person sales will form the backbone of the selling effort. Volunteers and helpers should be organized into competing teams vying to outsell one another, with prizes going to the most successful teams and individual salespersons.

Time: Planning for this fundraiser can be completed within a week. Delivery of the towels can take up to 3 to 4 weeks after ordering, depending upon the complexity of the design (insignia or logo) of the towel. An orientation session of 2 to 3 hours is held to educate volunteers and staff in the art of selling the towels. Allow 4 to 5 weeks of concentrated effort using both the point-of-sale and take-order methods of selling the merchandise. Of course, the selling of towels can continue indefinitely until all are sold.

Expenditures: Plan to spend $100 on promotional and publicity efforts. Some wholesalers require either a down payment or payment in full before the towels are shipped, depending upon the reputation of the sponsoring organization, its location in relation to the wholesaler, and the amount of money and the number of towels involved.

Personnel (Staff and Volunteers): Many young and adult volunteers (30-50) and a small staff (1-3) can form a formidable sales force. Adults should always be in charge of handling the payments, depositing the funds in the bank, and accounting for both the inventory and the cash on hand.

RISK MANAGEMENT

There is less risk involved when sales are made on a take-order basis, because the merchandise is not ordered until the orders have been taken. Using the point-of-sale concept, the sponsoring organization anticipates how many towels can be sold within a reasonable amount of time and then gambles by purchasing an inventory of merchandise. Many sponsoring organizations combine both selling methods in an effort to diminish the overall risk in terms of unsold merchandise languishing in storage.

PERMITS/LICENSES

If salespersons plan to go door-to-door, the group may need to obtain a peddler's permit from the community in which the canvassing will take place. Check with the town clerk or other municipal offices to see if such a license or permit is necessary.

HINTS

The sponsoring organization should hold a training session to teach both adult and young volunteers how to sell. There should never be any aggressive sales tactics involved. For youngsters, emphasize the safety aspects of selling, especially when going door-to-door. Purchasers will buy one or more towels for two major reasons: (1) the towels prove to be a good buy in terms of price and quality, and (2) the merchandise is being sold by a nonprofit organization to support a worthy cause.

Halloween Haunted
Hayrides

POTENTIAL NET INCOME

$6,000

COMPLEXITY/DEGREE OF DIFFICULTY

Moderate

DESCRIPTION

The sponsoring organization arranges hayrides on flatbed trailers drawn by tractors. The route is decorated to create a "frighteningly fun" experience. Scary goblins, ghosts, and witches await the travelers along the trail, ready to jump out and join the riders. Eerie sounds come from the trees and brush along the hayride's course. A hair-raising time is had by all! A concession stand is available at the start of the hayride and midway along the route. Tickets are priced at $5 for adults and $2 for children.

SCHEDULING

The Halloween Haunted Hayrides are promoted as part of the Halloween festivities throughout the month of October.

RESOURCES

Facilities: A portion of land is needed with gently sloping hills over which a trail can be blazed through trees and densely populated brush. The site should be within easy driving distance (perhaps 30 miles) of a major population center. Adequate parking is needed.

Equipment and Supplies: Flatbed trailers, tractors, hay, blankets, witch and ghost costumes, decorations, eerie music on audiocassettes or compact discs, portable compact disc or tape players, a suitable outdoor sound system, outdoor spotlights, a portable phone (for emergencies), portable generators or access to electricity, concession inventory (coffee, hot chocolate, donuts, cider, apples, and cookies), signs, a first-aid kit, a cash box, a receipt book, and a record book are needed.

Publicity and Promotion: Publicity for the hayrides can commence in late September and continue through Halloween. The rides are promoted as a family affair suitable for "kids of all ages." Announce that group rides at discount prices will be scheduled by appointment. All riders, as well as the public, should be made aware that the hayrides are sponsored by a worthy nonprofit organization and that the money raised will be put to good use within the community. Paid advertisements and news releases can be helpful in making the Halloween Haunted Hayrides a success. Announce the event in local advertising periodicals, and display signs at various business locations. Establish advance-sale ticket outlets in the community. Announce the hay rides at other events sponsored by the organizers and by other groups. Position large, temporary signs along the roadside near the start of the hayride.

Time: Allow 2 to 3 weeks for planning this fundraiser. The rides are conducted from late September through Halloween. Allow 30 minutes each to set up for each day's hayrides and to clean up following the last ride. Each ride lasts around 30 minutes. If three different flatbed trailers and tractors are available, the rides can start off every 20 minutes.

Expenditures: Plan to spend $100 for the concession inventory and $300 for promotional expenses. Everything else (including the use of the land, flatbed trailers, and tractors) should be obtained without cost to the sponsoring group. Have $100 in change available each evening.

Personnel (Staff and Volunteers): Many volunteers (25-30) and a small staff (1-2) are needed to drive the tractors that pull the trailers over the "haunted trail" and to be stationed, in costume, along the route. Each driver can be dressed as a ghost, witch, or warlock. All helpers are scheduled on a rotating basis so that no one works more than 3 to 4 hours at a stretch. Additional volunteers (5-7) are assigned tasks relating to the promotion and publicity surrounding the hayrides. Helpers (10-15) also are needed to operate the concession stand and to sell tickets at the site.

RISK MANAGEMENT

There must be adequate insurance coverage for the owner of the land. The sponsoring group's umbrella insurance policy should cover the volunteers and staff working the event. Check with the appropriate insurance companies to make sure that sufficient coverage is in place. Only experienced and skilled tractor operators should be allowed to drive the tractors. Anticipate that injuries may occur; have an emergency plan of action in place, including a readily available list of emergency phone numbers, a portable phone, and a volunteer on duty who is certified in first aid.

PERMITS/LICENSES

Some communities require a special food permit for the operation of any kind of concession stand. Check with the appropriate municipal office or the department of health. Follow all applicable regulations regarding the storage, preparation, and dispensation of food and drink.

HINTS

Once successful, the Halloween Haunted Hayride could become a highly anticipated annual event.

Affinity Credit Card Sponsorship

POTENTIAL NET INCOME

$6,000 annually

COMPLEXITY/DEGREE OF DIFFICULTY

Moderate

DESCRIPTION

The nonprofit group makes arrangements with an area bank to sponsor an affinity national credit card, either a Visa card or a Mastercard. The credit card is decorated with the logo of the sponsoring organization and provides the organization with a small percentage of the amounts charged on the cards. This percentage is determined by the amount of interest charged by the bank for the use of the credit cards. Friends and supporters of the sponsoring organization, as well as members of the public, are encouraged to apply for this affinity credit card. Depending upon the caliber of the sponsoring group, the attractiveness of the credit cards, the interest rate, and the amount of money charged by the patrons on the credit cards, the net profit on an annual basis easily can reach $6,000.

SCHEDULING

This fundraising project can be initiated at any time of the year.

RESOURCES

Facilities: An office is needed in which the volunteers can prepare solicitation letters.

Equipment and Supplies: Stationery, envelopes, stamps, and posters are necessary. A borrowed computer and laser printer are necessary to prepare the letters of solicitation.

Publicity and Promotion: Announcements of the availability of the affinity credit cards can be made through the area newspapers and advertising periodicals, and through personalized solicitation letters sent to friends and boosters of the sponsoring organization. The bank issuing the credit cards can send applications to those people whose names are provided by the sponsoring organization and to a host of other potential card users. Use the public-address system at other events sponsored by the fundraising group to publicize the availability of the credit cards. Promote the cards as an ongoing fundraising effort for the nonprofit organization.

Time: This fundraising project can be planned within 2 weeks. Making arrangements with the bank can take 4 to 5 weeks. Allow 3 months for the marketing activities to generate successful credit applications from individuals. Anticipate waiting 9 months before any income is realized, and up to 12 months before a consistent flow of money is established.

Expenditures: Plan to spend less than $50 for promotional efforts, stationery, envelopes, and stamps.

Personnel (Staff and Volunteers): The affinity credit card project can be started through the efforts of a small number of volunteers (5-7) and staff (1-2). A volunteer who is a lawyer or accountant, or who is a person of influence in the community, would be invaluable in working out the details with the bank.

RISK MANAGEMENT

There is no financial risk or liability exposure involved in this fundraising effort.

PERMITS/LICENSES

None

HINTS

This type of fundraising effort is only appropriate if the sponsoring organization has a sufficiently large base of supporters to justify the bank's time and effort to initiate an affinity credit card program for that group.

45

Licensed Merchandise and Apparel Sales

POTENTIAL NET INCOME

$6,000 annually

COMPLEXITY/DEGREE OF DIFFICULTY

Moderate

DESCRIPTION

The sport or recreation organization registers its trademark, logo, or unique name through the United States government and then arranges to sell merchandise and apparel on which its licensed and protected logos and various sport symbols are affixed. The group can either sell the items itself or can subcontract with one of several national organizations that specifically exist to aid sport and related groups market their licensed merchandise. Profit on licensed merchandise sold by the organization itself can range from 20 percent to 40 percent of the selling price, depending upon the item sold. If licensed apparel is sold by a professional marketing company, the royalty can range from 4 percent to 7 percent of the selling price. Almost anything can be sold as merchandise with a licensed logo, symbol, or unique name affixed (e.g., shirts, caps, cups, bumper stickers). However, not everything sold by the organization must have a licensed logo or symbol attached. An organization can successfully market and sell unlicensed apparel with only its name on the item.

SCHEDULING

The process of registering a logo, trademark, symbol, and so forth can be initiated at any time. You don't need an attorney to do this. The forms are simple and straightforward. The marketing and selling of the merchandise on which logos or symbols are attached likewise can be started at any time. If the items are to be sold by the sponsoring organization itself, a special event tied to the "initial availability" of the merchandise provides excellent visibility for the goods and high first-day sales and profits.

RESOURCES

Facilities: If the fundraising group will be selling its own merchandise, a site must be secured where the items can be displayed and sold. A storage site is necessary for unsold merchandise.

Equipment and Supplies: Display tables, price tags, receipt books, record books, cash boxes, displays, and signs are needed.

Publicity and Promotion: Both licensed and unlicensed merchandise can be sold by the sponsoring organization at its events and facility. Items also can be sold by area merchants, although a smaller profit is generated by the organization. Sales of items can be specifically organized around a particular theme or period of time, such as the soccer season or Christmas. All merchandise should be marketed on the basis of quality, style, attractiveness, and mass appeal to fans and to the general public. Emphasize that all profits go to a worthy cause sponsored by the organization.

Time: A merchandising plan can be organized within 2 to 3 weeks. Completing the application for government registration of a unique trademark, logo, slogan, symbol, or name can take up to 6 or 8 weeks. Selecting, ordering, and receiving the merchandise can take another 4 to 6 weeks. The selling window can range from 3 to 4 weeks or selling can be done on an ongoing basis.

Expenditures: Plan to spend $750 for inventory and for supplies needed to sell the items and to record the sales.

Personnel (Staff and Volunteers): Several volunteers (10-15) and a small staff (1-2) are needed to select, order, store, and market the items to be sold. Solicit an additional sales force of 15-25 volunteers.

RISK MANAGEMENT

The greatest risk involved is having merchandise that no one wants to buy. To prevent this catastrophe, the organizers must be cautious about the items they order, including the style and color of those items, as well as the quantity. Better to order small quantities (even at higher cost per item) and then reorder when necessary than to end up with a large inventory of unsold merchandise. Of course, the more popular the sponsoring organization, the greater the marketability of the merchandise.

Financial accountability requires that accurate records be kept of all inventory, sales, and cash received. Careful controls should be put into place to account for all merchandise and profits.

PERMITS/LICENSES

Check with the town clerk to see if the organization needs to obtain a peddler's license to sell items at events.

HINTS

Whenever a sport or recreation group has a popular and unique trademark, logo, slogan, mascot, symbol, or name, the organizers should obtain appropriate licensing (registration) under the 1989 Trademark Law Revision Act. Contact the Commissioner of Patents and Trademarks, "Box Trademark," Washington, DC 20231 (703-308-4357) to request information and the appropriate forms. Only with such licensing will the organization have legal protection against unauthorized use of its unique name or symbol on items or for other use.

Bowl-a-Thon

POTENTIAL NET INCOME

$6,000

COMPLEXITY/DEGREE OF DIFFICULTY

Moderate

DESCRIPTION

Youngsters and adults seek pledges for the pins they will knock down at a local bowling event. Each participant will bowl three games. Sponsors may donate various amounts (2 cents, 10 cents, or more) for each pin knocked down by the soliciting individual with the first ball in each frame. Donations also can be pledged for each strike made by that bowler. The bowling party also involves competition among the volunteer bowlers (categorized by age groups, prior experience, and skill levels). Volunteers provide free drinks and sandwiches. Ribbons and trophies for individual and team performances are awarded to the participants.

SCHEDULING

This fundraising project can be scheduled whenever the participants and the bowling alley are available. Weekends are ideal.

RESOURCES

Facilities: Almost any bowling alley will do.

Equipment and Supplies: Pledge sheets and posters are necessary. Decorations, prizes, sandwiches, and drinks are needed for the bowling party. Bowling balls, shoes, and scorecards are provided by the bowling alley.

Publicity and Promotion: Promotional efforts center around newspaper coverage of the upcoming event and public-service announcements provided by radio and television stations. Display posters at the sites of local businesses and organizations. Use the public-address system at other events sponsored by the organization and at events sponsored by other groups.

An important aspect of promotion involves person-to-person soliciting. How the volunteers present themselves while seeking pledges will significantly affect the prospective donors' impression of the fundraising project and the sponsoring organization. A training session should be held to instruct the bowlers how to approach prospective contributors. Solicitors should emphasize that this fundraiser is being sponsored by a nonprofit group and that the profit will be put to a worthy cause in the community.

Time: The Bowl-a-Thon can be planned within a week. Reserve the bowling lanes at least 6 weeks in advance. Solicitation of pledges should be limited to 3 or 4 weeks. The bowling party will take approximately 3 hours. Plan on an additional hour to prepare for the bowling party, then another hour to clean up afterward. Collection of the money pledged can be concluded over a weekend.

Expenditures: This fundraising project can be initiated for less than $50 for publicity purposes. The food and drink, prizes, decorations, and use of the bowling alley should be donated. If these cannot be obtained for free, the organization must find a generous benefactor who will pay the expenses.

Personnel (Staff and Volunteers): The larger the number of bowlers seeking pledges, the greater the likelihood of financial success. At least 45 should participate. Additional adult volunteers (7-10) and staff (1-2) are needed to plan and implement this fundraiser, including making arrangements with the bowling alley to use the facility without cost. These volunteers also are needed to promote this fun-filled event.

RISK MANAGEMENT

There are no financial risks involved in this fundraiser. Liability exposure is minimal as long as all safety rules for bowling are followed. The training session should educate the bowlers about the safety rules for bowling.

PERMITS/LICENSES

Some communities require a peddlers' permit for solicitors to go door-to-door seeking pledges. Check with the town clerk or other municipal offices in your community.

HINTS

Some organizers involve adults and youngsters in the bowling party but send only the youngsters to solicit pledges; other organizations allow adults and youngsters to seek donations; still other groups limit the bowling participation to youngsters. Your organization's circumstances will determine how you structure this event. A brief introductory bowling lesson should be provided for those who do not know how to bowl. In order not to surprise (and cause ill feelings with) potential donors, the soliciting bowlers should allow the donors to specify the maximum amount that might be contributed. Avoid a situation in which an individual pledges 30 cents a pin, only to find out that this translates into a $72 contribution. Plan to collect 88 percent to 90 percent of the money pledged.

Community Afghan Sale

POTENTIAL NET INCOME
$6,363

COMPLEXITY/DEGREE OF DIFFICULTY
Moderate

DESCRIPTION
Unique and colorful afghans, measuring 50 inches by 65 inches, are sold to commemorate 6 to 10 historical buildings or landmarks in the community. Each afghan is 100 percent cotton and is machine washable and dryable. They are available in a variety of colors, including custom colors. The afghans are manufactured by Riddle Manufacturing, Inc., P.O. Box 2058, Burlington, North Carolina 27216 (800-327-9270). When ordering, organizers should submit one or more photos or drawings of each of the local buildings or sites to be depicted. Several border designs are available. Thus, there will be a personalized and creative touch to the afghan that is unique to the community.

SCHEDULING
The sale of the afghans may be initiated at any time. The selling period should extend until all of the afghans are sold.

RESOURCES
Facilities: A room must be available where unsold afghans can be stored. Various business sites in the area can serve as sales outlets.

Equipment and Supplies: Photographs and drawings of the sites, a cash box, a record book, a receipt book, and afghans are essential for this fundraiser.

Publicity and Promotion: Place advertisements (including photos of the afghans) in area newspapers and advertising periodicals. Local radio stations might provide free advertising as part of their public-service announcements. Put signs at various businesses and organizations, which might also serve as selling sites. A couple of organizers can publicize their home phone numbers in order to take orders by telephone. Prospective purchasers can be approached on a person-to-person basis, via telephone or face-to-face. Sample afghans should be displayed at some prominent locales in the community, such as the hospital, the museum, the library, and the Chamber of Commerce. Promote the fact that this is a fundraising effort sponsored by a local, nonprofit organization. Highlight how the profits will be put to good use.

Time: This fundraiser can be planned within a few weeks. Producing photographs or creating the drawings can take considerably longer. Allocate 4 months to create the final designs and another 2 months for the afghans to be produced. The manufacturer will create a first and second draft of each design; then a computer printout is produced.

A sample afghan is sent to the sponsoring organization prior to the production of the order.

Expenditures: This fundraising project can be started for $150, mainly for promotional and publicity efforts. There are two types of afghans that can be ordered. The wholesale cost of the two-layer afghan is $21 apiece, with a suggested retail price of between $44.95 and $49.95. The two-and-a-half layer afghan wholesales at $25.50 and retails between $54.99 and $59.99 each. There is a minimum initial order of 225 afghans and a minimum reorder of 50. Freight is paid by the fundraising group.

Personnel (Staff and Volunteers): Volunteers (5-10) and staff (1-2) are needed to plan and implement the Community Afghan Sale.

RISK MANAGEMENT

There is no significant liability exposure associated with this fundraising effort. To reduce the financial risk, organizers should attempt to presell as many afghans as possible. Dealing with an experienced manufacturer reduces the risk of unsatisfactory merchandise.

PERMITS/LICENSES

None

HINTS

The afghans make memorable and unique gifts. They also are suitable for people to purchase for themselves to display in their homes.

Photos With Life-Size Stand-Up Stars

POTENTIAL NET INCOME

$6,750 annually

COMPLEXITY/DEGREE OF DIFFICULTY

Low

DESCRIPTION

A 6-foot color stand-up cutout of a famous individual (e.g., Bugs Bunny, Superman, John Wayne) is used as a prop for photo shoots. Patrons pay $10 (or whatever the market will bear) for each souvenir photo taken with the "celebrity." The photographs are taken with a Polaroid camera, thus allowing for immediate delivery to the customer and immediate payment. With the organization's cost of the

individual pictures being around 50 cents to 90 cents, the profit will be more than $9 per photo. The sponsors can expect to average 15 photos, therefore about $135, per event. If there are 50 events during the year, the organization would realize a net profit of over $6,750.

SCHEDULING

The life-size cutouts are displayed at various sporting contests and recreational events, thus taking advantage of a large crowd of potential customers.

RESOURCES

Facilities: Almost any indoor or outdoor site that has high foot traffic will do. For example, the cutout and photographer can be stationed near the stands or close to the concessions at a football or field hockey game, inside a recreation hall, in a basketball gymnasium, or even in the hallway adjacent to the ticket booth leading to an event.

Equipment and Supplies: Professionally created stand-up cutouts can be purchased from several commercial sources. One such company is Advanced Graphics, P.O. Box 8517, Pittsburgh, California 94565-8517 (510-432-2262). The Polaroid camera can either be borrowed or purchased. A plentiful supply of Polaroid film must be on hand. It is better to have too much film than not enough. A table, cash box, and $50 in change are needed.

Publicity and Promotion: The cutouts serve as the best promotion for this fundraiser. One or more standups prominently displayed will attract a great deal of attention. One means of gaining and retaining the interest of potential purchasers is to use cutouts of several famous individuals at different times of the year and to have more than one cutout available at any one time. Having several different types of cutouts means that the promoters will have a character to interest almost every potential customer. To further promote sales, publicize the nonprofit nature of the sponsoring group and the purpose for which the money is being raised.

Time: Planning for this fundraiser can be completed within a week. The time between ordering the cutouts and delivery will be 2 to 3 weeks. The photo opportunity sessions can range from 30 minutes to the duration of the athletic contest or special event.

Expenditures: Prices for life-size stand-up cutouts vary between $25 and $35 per. Buy film at discount stores or through bulk purchases. Plan to spend less than $100 to get started and around $500 annually.

Personnel (Staff and Volunteers): A few volunteers and staff (2-4) are needed to solicit customers and assist in posing customers for the photographs.

RISK MANAGEMENT

No significant risks are involved.

PERMITS/LICENSES

If the photos are to be taken at a school or on the recreation organization's own site, there is no need for a special permit or license. If the photos are to be taken on public streets or sidewalks, a permit might be required. Check with the town clerk or bureau of licenses in the municipality where the photo sessions will take place.

HINTS

The sponsoring organization might want to charge less money per picture in order to attract more business and earn greater overall profits. Another tactic is to take the cutout to different sites, such as schools and businesses, to solicit photo purchases. An arrangement might be made to deliver a cutout to an event (e.g., party, dance, picnic) and take pictures for a reduced charge (perhaps $5 per) if a stipulated number of photo sales (say, 50) is guaranteed.

Magazine Sales

POTENTIAL NET INCOME
$7,000

COMPLEXITY/DEGREE OF DIFFICULTY
Moderate

DESCRIPTION
Volunteers for the nonprofit group solicit magazine subscriptions and renewals on behalf of a magazine distribution company. The sponsoring organization keeps 40 percent to 50 percent of the total sales. There are numerous magazine subscription companies that operate in this fashion. One is Q.S.P., 4467 Shady Ridge Drive, Hamburg, NY 14075 (716-648-0178). The selling territory is usually restricted to the organization's own community. The customer base includes individuals, organizations, and companies. Money for the magazines is collected at the time that the order is taken. The magazines will be delivered to the customers within 6 weeks.

SCHEDULING
The sale of magazine subscriptions can take place at any time of the year. However, selling door-to-door is always easiest and safest in nice weather.

RESOURCES
Facilities: A room is needed in which to plan this fundraiser and to conduct a training session for those volunteers who will be canvassing the community.

Equipment and Supplies: The sponsoring organization supplies promotional signs and flyers. Order forms and promotional brochures can be obtained from the wholesaler that provides the magazines.

Publicity and Promotion: The subscription campaign should be publicized in local newspapers and advertising periodicals. Announcements should be made at other events of the sponsoring organization. When canvassing, solicitors should bring along promotional flyers that they can show or leave with potential customers. Parents and other relatives of youngsters involved in the campaign can solicit subscriptions from friends and coworkers. In this way the selling area is tremendously expanded and the potential for big dollars in profits greatly enhanced. Tell all potential purchasers that this is a fundraising project conducted by a local, nonprofit organization; also relate how the money will be put to good use within the community.

Time: This fundraiser can be planned within a week. Making final arrangements with, and securing order forms and promotional materials from, a suitable subscription company might take 2 to 3 weeks. Keep the selling window for the subscriptions and renewals to a maximum of 3 or 4 weeks.

Expenditures: This fundraiser can be initiated for less than $100 in promotional expenses.

Personnel (Staff and Volunteers): Assuming that the salespersons (youngsters and adults) have been suitably trained and are highly motivated, a sales force of 50 to 75 people can reap big financial dividends with a minimum of effort and risk. Establish a committee to oversee the solicitation effort, the handling of the money, and other details of the operation.

RISK MANAGEMENT

There is no real financial risk in this project. The legal exposure is diminished by holding a training session for the youngsters and adults who will be involved in selling subscriptions. Youngsters must be instructed to solicit in pairs and not to go door-to-door at night or in strange neighborhoods without being accompanied by an adult. Additionally, all salespersons must be instructed not to use the hard-sell approach.

PERMITS/LICENSES

Many communities now require door-to-door solicitors to obtain a peddler's permit. Check with your town clerk or other municipal offices.

HINTS

Be sure to select a company that offers a wide range of popular magazines. This selection greatly increases the possibility that customers will find a magazine to which they would like to subscribe. The manner in which the magazines are sold is very important. No group wants a reputation of being pushy when soliciting funds. More harm than good would result.

Street Fund Drive

POTENTIAL NET INCOME

$7,500

COMPLEXITY/DEGREE OF DIFFICULTY

Low

DESCRIPTION

Older teenagers and adults are strategically stationed near stoplights to collect donations from motorists. The solicitors wear special T-shirts and hats and display promotional signs so that drivers can recognize from a distance that the volunteers represent a worthwhile organization. (If athletes are involved, they may wear their uniforms instead of the T-shirts and hats.) Carrying decorated coffee cans in which to collect the contributions, the solicitors walk carefully along the drivers' side of the cars when the motorists stop at the intersection.

SCHEDULING

This fundraiser can be held on any day when there is heavy traffic. Saturdays often are very productive. The weather must be nice so that drivers will have their vehicles' windows down, thus being more approachable. The soliciting effort can be accomplished on a single day or may be extended to 2 or more days.

RESOURCES

Facilities: Solicitors should be stationed at four to eight intersections.

Equipment and Supplies: Posters, decorated coffee cans, T-shirts and hats (or team uniforms), and borrowed safety vests are required.

Publicity and Promotion: Send announcements to local newspapers and advertising periodicals, and display posters at area business sites. Radio and television stations might promote this fundraiser as part of their public-service announcements. Use the public-address systems at community activities and competitive sport contests. Highlight the nonprofit nature of the sponsoring entity, and reveal how the money raised will be put to good use within the community.

Time: This fundraiser can be organized within a week. Training of the solicitors can be completed in 1 to 2 hours. Volunteers can be scheduled to work three 3- to 4-hour shifts from 7 A.M. until 6 P.M.

Expenditures: Plan to spend less than $100 for promotional purposes, T-shirts, and hats.

Personnel (Staff and Volunteers): The sponsoring organization will need a minimum of 96 solicitors if six intersections are worked.

RISK MANAGEMENT

Although there is no financial risk in this project, there is always the danger of a volunteer being struck by a vehicle. The organizers would be wise to restrict solicitors to adults (ages 18 and older) and require that these volunteers sign an agreement that releases the sponsoring organization from liability in the event of an accident. The organizers should instruct the solicitors how to maneuver safely through the traffic near the intersections, and the volunteers must wear bright clothing. If the solicitors are athletes, they can wear bright vests over their uniforms.

PERMITS/LICENSES

A peddler's permit might be required in some communities. In other communities, permission must be obtained from the local police authority.

HINTS

To provide good public relations between the sponsoring organization and the community, the volunteers must solicit in a polite, friendly, and professional manner. This event can become a successful annual affair, with the community expecting the street intersection solicitation.

Date Auction and Dinner

POTENTIAL NET INCOME

$7,500

COMPLEXITY/DEGREE OF DIFFICULTY

Moderate

DESCRIPTION

To raise money for a worthy cause, the nonprofit organization auctions dates with 75 local professional and celebrity men. The men bring equipment items that hint as to the type of activity that will comprise the date or excursion (e.g., skis, a cowboy hat, tickets to a special event). Prior to the auction, a formal dinner is held for the participants. The admission price for the dinner is set to generate a $30 profit over the cost of the meal and the rental of the facility. Thus, if 150 women attend, the initial net profit would be $4,500. Add to this figure the income from the auction, and the total net profit from the evening's activities easily could reach $7,500.

SCHEDULING

The Date Auction and Dinner can be scheduled at any time of the year.

RESOURCES

Facilities: The sponsoring organization must secure a site that can seat 150 guests for dinner and accommodate a portable stage. Adequate and safe parking is a must. Although a facility belonging to the organization may be used, a restaurant or party house might be preferred in order to facilitate the evening's activities and to provide the desired atmosphere.

Equipment and Supplies: Food and drink for the meal is provided by the facility hosting the dinner and is paid for out of the profits. The organization provides additional tables, tablecloths, and chairs; signs; decorations; a cash box; receipt books; tickets; and a high-quality sound system with a portable microphone.

Publicity and Promotion: Publicity surrounding the advance sale of admission tickets should be centered around announcements and advertisements in the local media (don't forget the advertising periodicals), signs displayed in local merchants' stores, and word of mouth. Announcements can be made over the public-address systems at other events sponsored by the organizing group. Advance tickets can be sold door-to-door, through the mail, at local businesses, and through personal contacts. Let everyone know that this fundraiser is being sponsored by a nonprofit organization and that the profits will go toward a worthy cause within the community.

Time: The dinner and auction can be planned within 3 weeks. Allow 3 to 4 weeks to line up the men who will agree to be "auctioned." The advertising and promotional (ticket selling) activities should take less than 3 or 4 weeks.

Expenditures: The dinner will cost the organization between $20 and $30 per person. Allocate $200 for promotional and publicity efforts. A professional auctioneer might be found who will serve pro bono due to the nonprofit nature of the event; otherwise, expect to spend $250 for the services of a top-notch professional for this job.

Personnel (Staff and Volunteers): Several volunteers (15-20) and a small staff (2-3) are needed to plan the event, promote the auction and dinner, and sell the tickets. The auctioneer must be a professional. In lieu of an auctioneer, a popular master of ceremonies might suffice, although much would be lost in the sense of spontaneity and urgency that an auctioneer would provide. The organization must obtain commitments from a large number of men (45-65) who are willing to participate as the dates to be auctioned.

RISK MANAGEMENT

The greatest risk to which the planners are exposed is the inability to sell sufficient advance tickets to make this a truly big money maker. Thus, boosters and friends of the sponsoring group must not only purchase the tickets but also play a significant role in selling tickets to their friends, family members, and coworkers. If the event is held at the organization's own facility, the liability exposure is diminished if regulations pertaining to the storage, handling, preparation, and serving of food are adhered to. Confirm that the facility's blanket insurance policy provides adequate coverage for this type of fundraising event.

PERMITS/LICENSES

If the auction and dinner are held at a restaurant or party house, there is no need for any special licenses or permits. However, if the event is to be held in a gymnasium, a large field house, or other such facility, the organizers may need to obtain a special food license for this event.

HINTS

Advance ticket sales are essential so that the organizers can plan for an accurate number of meals to be ordered.

52 Indoor Winter Walkabout

POTENTIAL NET INCOME
$7,500

COMPLEXITY/DEGREE OF DIFFICULTY
Moderate

DESCRIPTION
In the middle of winter, volunteers of all ages walk 10 laps around the inside of an area mall. The laps can be completed within an hour. Profits are generated from donations (10 cents to $1 or more per lap) obtained in advance (not pledged) from individual and business donors by the walkers-to-be. On the day of the Indoor Winter Walkabout, the volunteers bring the donations to the mall to give to the sponsoring organization. At the end of the walkabout, donated prizes are awarded to the volunteers who collected the most contributions, and donated refreshments are available to the walkers and organizers. Then, all of the participants are treated to a free movie.

SCHEDULING
This fundraiser should be scheduled for January or February, when the weather is coldest and most dreary. The Indoor Winter Walkabout is especially effective in areas where snow, wind, and extremely cold temperatures dominate the winter months.

RESOURCES
Facilities: The organizers locate a large mall for this event.

Equipment and Supplies: Sponsor forms, liability releases, a receipt book, a record book, flyers, posters, refreshments, a portable public-address system, door prizes, decorations, tables, chairs, first-aid kits, thank-you cards, envelopes, and stamps are required.

Publicity and Promotion: The news media should be approached to provide free publicity for this worthy, nonprofit fundraising project. Local businesses and organizations can display signs and posters announcing the walkabout. Sponsor forms should be distributed to numerous organizations and businesses in an effort to solicit volunteer walkers and contributions in the form of money, goods, and services. Person-to-person (both face-to-face and via the phone) solicitation of potential walkers and contributions is essential to the success of the Indoor Winter Walkabout.

Time: This fundraising project can be planned within a week. Securing sufficient volunteers as walkers will take 2 or 3 weeks, and the solicitation and receipt of donations should be completed within 4 weeks. The volunteers walk from 9:30 to 10:30 A.M. on a Sunday or at another time when the mall normally is closed. Check-in time is 8:30 A.M. The walkabout should be over by 11:30 A.M. The special showing of the free movie for the participants and donors follows immediately.

Expenditures: Plan to spend $150 to initiate this project. Most of the supplies (e.g., prizes, stamps, forms) can be obtained on a donated or loan basis due to the nonprofit nature of the event. The use of the mall and the movie theater must be obtained without cost.

Personnel (Staff and Volunteers): The success of this project depends upon the large number of volunteers (100-150) needed to take part in the walk. Other volunteers (5-7) and staff (1-2) are needed to plan and organize this fundraiser. A nurse or athletic trainer should be at the mall in case of an accident or illness among the volunteers. Volunteers should not be restricted to members of the sponsoring organization. Anyone from the community can volunteer. Expanding the volunteer base in this way is one of the keys to financial success in this fundraiser.

RISK MANAGEMENT

Each adult walker should sign a liability release. Such a document absolves the sponsoring organization, the mall proprietors, and the individuals involved from liability, other than for gross negligence. For those youngsters taking part, parents or guardians should sign a liability release and permission agreement. There is no financial risk involved in this type of fundraising effort.

PERMITS/LICENSES

Permission must be obtained well in advance from the management of the mall where the walkabout will take place.

HINTS

The fact that the donations are collected in advance eliminates the need for the volunteer walkers to return to the donors to pick up the contributions. Following the walkabout, the organization sends each donor a personal thank-you note in appreciation of the contribution and to confirm that the individual volunteer did indeed complete the necessary laps. Special corporate sponsors should be sought, and their contributions can take the form of cash, services, and goods.

Annual Fundraising Campaign

POTENTIAL NET INCOME
$7,500 annually

COMPLEXITY/DEGREE OF DIFFICULTY
Moderate

DESCRIPTION
This fundraising effort involves an annual fundraising solicitation of donations for a specific and easily supported purpose. The solicitations are made by letter, telephone, or face-to-face contact. The contributions can be used for any recurring, worthwhile cause, such as sending needy youths to summer camp or purchasing new uniforms for the various youth sport teams. All of the money collected will be spent that year for the purpose stated.

SCHEDULING
Although the fundraising campaign may be initiated during any month, the renewal should begin each year at the same time.

RESOURCES
Facilities: The organization must establish an office in which to hold meetings, make phone calls, prepare mailings, and receive contributions.

Equipment and Supplies: Signs, stationery, envelopes, pledge cards, return envelopes, and stamps are necessary. Arrangements must be made for the use of phones, a computer, a laser printer, and the appropriate word processing and graphic software.

Publicity and Promotion: Promotional and publicity efforts are aimed toward those individuals, organizations, and businesses most likely to contribute to a worthwhile and recurring cause. Signs should be displayed by various businesses and organizations, some of which may serve as collection sites for donations. Announcements in the area news media are critical. Mass mailings are made to supporters, fans, vendors, past contributors, and all others deemed likely to be sympathetic to the cause for which the money is being sought. Those persons in the organization who are particularly influential should make phone calls or personal visits to prime prospects.

After the initial Annual Fundraising Campaign is over and the money raised and spent, take photos of the kids at camp or in their new uniforms to send to the area newspapers and television stations. Ask the editors and managers to run human interest stories about the event. Prior to subsequent campaigns, send more photos to the media in anticipation that publicity will be provided prior to the renewed solicitation effort.

Time: Organizing this event can take 1 to 2 weeks. The solicitation period should be limited to 4 to 6 weeks.

Expenditures: Plan to spend $350 on promotional and publicity efforts, including office supplies and mailing expenses. The use of office equipment can usually be obtained on a free or loan basis because of the nonprofit nature of the sponsoring entity and the worthwhile purpose of the fundraising endeavor. Don't spend if you don't have to.

Personnel (Staff and Volunteers): A moderate-sized group of dedicated volunteers (15-20) and a small staff (1-2) can effectively run this type of annual campaign, especially in subsequent years after they've gained experience with this fundraiser.

RISK MANAGEMENT

There are no significant financial or liability risks involved with this annual campaign. Be sure, however, that this effort does not conflict with other fundraising projects sponsored by the organization. Conducting more than one major fundraiser at the same time tends to annoy potential donors and drain them of their generosity. Implementing concurrent fundraisers also stretches one's staff and volunteers to their limits or beyond.

PERMITS/LICENSES

None

HINTS

The first year of the Annual Fundraising Campaign will be the most challenging. At this time, it is new to the public and to those attempting to make it a success. For the sake of the renewals of this fundraiser, the initial campaign must be well-organized and expertly implemented, and must end up an enormous success. Once the community and contributors are aware of the purpose of the campaign and its success in meeting a worthy goal within the community, subsequent campaigns will be much easier to pull off.

The essential element of the annual campaign is the purpose for which the campaign is conducted every year. The organizers must select a truly worthwhile and popular need that will exist year after year. The Annual Fundraising Campaign should be used to solicit large amounts of money in each donation. An organization would not want to use such a vehicle as the Annual Fundraising Campaign to solicit nickels and dimes. The substantial level of financial assistance solicited should be an amount that can be sustained by the pool of contributors.

One Million Pennies

POTENTIAL NET INCOME

$9,800

COMPLEXITY/DEGREE OF DIFFICULTY

Low

DESCRIPTION

The collection of pennies in a suitable depository or container continues throughout the year until the publicized goal of 1 million pennies ($10,000) is reached.

SCHEDULING

The solicitation and collection of pennies can take place at any activity or event sponsored by the recreation or sport entity. The project may be initiated at any time.

RESOURCES

Facilities: No special facilities are necessary.

Equipment and Supplies: Attractive containers in which to collect the pennies are needed. On each container is an advertisement that promotes the fundraising effort. Tables or stands upon which to place the containers are needed. Large signs that succinctly outline the purpose of the fundraiser need to be created.

Publicity and Promotion: In addition to the small advertisements placed on each collection container, a large sign is put on the wall where each collection effort is stationed. The copy on these signs describes the nature of the project, highlights the nonprofit status of the sponsoring organization, and explains how the money raised will be put to good use. Securing strategic locations to display the collection containers and signs is very important. The most productive areas are near the ticket booths, beside the concession stand(s), and alongside the entrance to the facility. During each event at which the collection containers are displayed, announcements are made over the public-address system to relate that this worthwhile fundraising project is ongoing and that 1 million pennies are being sought. If appropriate, volunteers can pass containers through the crowd after an announcement to that effect is made by the announcer during a strategic break in the event's activities. The community can be made aware of this fundraising project through the news media and by signs displayed at the sites of area businesses and organizations.

Time: This fundraiser can be planned in 1 or 2 days. The collection of pennies continues until the goal is reached.

Expenditures: Allocate $200 for the promotional signs and for the various collection containers. Tables can be obtained on a free or loan basis.

Personnel (Staff and Volunteers): There is a need for volunteers and staff (5-10) to help in the promotional activity and publicity associated with this fundraiser. One or 2 adults are assigned to each of the collection containers that are displayed at the various contests and events. Co-treasurers are accountable for depositing the monies in the bank and reporting the progress of the fundraising project.

RISK MANAGEMENT

There are no significant risks in terms of financial or liability exposure. However, organizers must ensure that there is strict accounting of all the monies collected. For this reason, only adults should be assigned as collectors of pennies.

PERMITS/LICENSES

None

HINTS

The collection of pennies also can take place at various business sites. If permission is granted, the containers may be stationed at community events not sponsored by the sport or recreation entity. Let people know that donations of U.S. coins other than pennies would be welcomed. In addition to the solicitation of pennies, promoters might think about appealing to individuals and businesses for larger sums of money to supplement the collection of pennies.

PART IV

FUNDRAISERS GENERATING OVER $10,000

Tree of Lights

POTENTIAL NET INCOME
$10,500

COMPLEXITY/DEGREE OF DIFFICULTY
Moderate

DESCRIPTION
In late November, lights are placed on a large Christmas tree located outside a highly visible facility (e.g., school, hospital) and are "sold" for $10 each in memory of a special person or event. There is a formal tree lighting ceremony in early December. Orders continue to be taken—and new lights turned on—until mid-January. On behalf of the donor, the organization sends an acknowledgment certificate to the person being honored or to the relatives of the deceased person being remembered. Each honored person's name or event is inscribed in a traditional "Lights Book" that can be read by the public within the building.

SCHEDULING
The official "lighting of the tree" ceremony is scheduled for December 1. The lights remain on until mid-January.

RESOURCES
Facilities: A site is needed for the Christmas tree. A living tree can be used if it is located near high vehicular or foot traffic. The organization must secure a room in which to store the lights, extension cords, and other paraphernalia from one year to the next.

Equipment and Supplies: Extension cords and numerous strings of large, colored Christmas lights are required. Envelopes, stamps, and nicely printed certificates must be obtained for sending acknowledgments. Large ladders and a cherry picker or front loader assist in the stringing of lights. A large outdoor sign is created, then erected near the Christmas tree.

Publicity and Promotion: Send timely announcements to the local news media, including advertising periodicals, explaining the Tree of Lights project. Send similar notices to local businesses and organizations. Display signs at area businesses, some of which may accept orders and money for the lights. The sign erected near the tree promotes the fundraiser and thanks in a general way those donors who contributed to the Tree of Lights.

Time: The planning of this fundraising project can take several weeks to complete. The "selling" of the individual lights should begin in early November and extend until mid-January. Near the end of November, plan to spend 6 hours stringing the tree with lights. Taking down the lights and packing them away could take another 6 hours.

Expenditures: Allocate at least $250 for promotional and publicity efforts. If the Christmas lights are not donated, they should be purchased at reduced cost. Plan to spend around $160 for 1,000 lights. The cherry picker or front loader used for stringing and removing the lights should be borrowed from the municipal offices or from a construction firm in your community. If a tree must be cut and moved to the display site, plan on spending up to $150 for a truly splendid specimen.

Personnel (Staff and Volunteers): Many volunteers (20-25) and a small staff (2-4) promote this fundraiser, take orders, mail the certificates, help decorate the tree, and later take down the lights. Specialized help may be needed for setting up the electrical system, operating the cherry picker, and stringing the tree.

RISK MANAGEMENT

This fundraising project involves no significant liability exposure. Be sure that the people setting up and taking down the tree and lights will be covered by the insurance policy of either the sponsoring organization or the facility on whose grounds the tree is to be located. The financial risk is minimal because the lights are not purchased until a substantial number of orders and money have been received.

PERMITS/LICENSES

None

HINTS

This project is an ideal annual fundraiser. During subsequent years the promoters should contact the previous contributors to request another contribution. With a majority of these donors reordering their lights, a sufficient number of new contributors can be easily solicited each year.

Nite at the Races

POTENTIAL NET INCOME
$11,000

COMPLEXITY/DEGREE OF DIFFICULTY
Moderate

DESCRIPTION
A fun-filled evening is held where participants wager on horse races as seen on 16mm film or videotape. The color films or tapes show actual races that are called by professional announcers. The odds are determined prior to each race. Race films or videotapes may be obtained from a commercial company that specializes in renting such films or tapes. One such company is A Nite at the Races, Inc., 2043 Jupiter Circle, Jupiter, Florida 33548 (407-747-3900).

   In addition to the races, donated gifts are raffled. Refreshments consist of a free sandwich buffet and a cash bar, with nonalcoholic beverages available. The profit is generated from the sale of tickets, cash bar, raffle, and a percentage (5 percent to 10 percent) of all money wagered. Tickets are priced to generate a net profit of at least $25 per person. This event can be piggybacked with other games of chance, such as blackjack or bingo, to provide greater interest and profit.

SCHEDULING
Nite at the Races can be scheduled for any Friday or Saturday evening.

RESOURCES
Facilities: The organization must secure an indoor facility large enough to hold 200 people and provide space for showing the races at one end of the room. A gymnasium or cafeteria would suffice. Adequate parking is necessary.

Equipment and Supplies: Tables, chairs, a film projector, and a large screen are needed. If videotapes are used, a videotape player and a

52-inch-screen television or 6 televisions with screens 25 inches or larger will be required. The rental kit includes everything necessary to play: souvenir programs, pari-mutuel tickets, a tote board poster, a precalculated payoff chart and instructions, and more. A public-address system and raffle items are necessary. Food and drink must be available.

Publicity and Promotion: Announcements should be placed in local newspapers, including advertising periodicals. Because this fundraising project is sponsored by a nonprofit entity, radio and television stations might include promotional mention of this event as part of their public-service announcements. Display signs at local businesses, some of which can serve as advance-sale ticket outlets. All publicity surrounding this fundraiser must emphasize the non-profit nature of the sponsoring organization and relate how the profits will be used.

Time: This fundraiser can be organized within 2 weeks. After ordering the films or tapes, allow 3 weeks for delivery. The festivities start at 6 P.M. and conclude around 11. Allow at least 1 hour for cleanup.

Expenditures: The rental fee for a kit of 6 races will range from $180 to $220 (plus tax, insurance, and charges for shipping and handling). More races may be ordered at an additional charge. Use of the facility should be free. The cost of the sandwich buffet will be $5 or less per person. Allow $100 for promotional and publicity efforts. The raffle items are donated. The entire evening's activities can be implemented for less than $1,400.

Personnel (Staff and Volunteers): Several volunteers (15-20) and a small staff (1-2) sell tickets (in advance and at the door) and obtain donated items for the raffle. Additional helpers (7-10) run the other games of chance (if any) and staff the bar and buffet. An entertaining master of ceremonies keeps the activities moving at the proper pace.

RISK MANAGEMENT

With the sale of advance tickets (priced $5 less than tickets at the door), the financial risks are reduced considerably. Liability exposure is held to a minimum through full compliance with local and state laws pertaining to gambling, the sale of alcohol, and the distribution of food. Check to ensure that the blanket insurance policy of the facility will cover the sponsoring entity as well as those people working the event.

PERMITS/LICENSES

Since this fundraising project revolves around gambling, be sure to comply with all local and state regulations. A food license and temporary liquor permit might be necessary for the buffet and bar.

HINTS

This is a very popular and exciting audience-participation activity. Participants need not be knowledgeable about racing in order to enjoy the evening. (Organizers may opt to rent films/tapes of greyhound or harness racing instead.) To gain greater insight into how to run this type of fundraiser, the organizers may attend a similar event held by another group. Since alcoholic beverages are sold, the bartenders must be strict about not selling alcohol to patrons who are not of legal drinking age or who have had enough to drink. Establish a designated-driver program for the evening, and post signs urging moderation in drink.

Discounting Tickets to Corporations and Businesses

POTENTIAL NET INCOME

$11,000 annually

COMPLEXITY/DEGREE OF DIFFICULTY

Moderate

DESCRIPTION

The administrators of an athletic team solicit business sponsors to purchase blocks of tickets to one or more of their events at a significant discount. These are tickets that normally would remain unsold for the events. Tickets to individual games or for the entire season may be included in the discount packages. The businesses then distribute the tickets as they see fit as a promotional gimmick. Some sponsors also give the tickets to employees as a fringe benefit. If a single business buys all of the available tickets as a block for a specific athletic event, that business becomes the *official sponsor* of that particular contest.

SCHEDULING

Sponsors are sought 4 to 5 weeks prior to the first game of the sport season for which the tickets are to be discounted.

RESOURCES

Facilities: This fundraiser is implemented from the office of the athletic administrators.

Equipment and Supplies: During the game, display banners and signs within the athletic facility to publicize the supporters for that event. Special tickets must be printed for the sponsors.

Publicity and Promotion: Explain to prospective sponsors how they can use the tickets to bolster business by giving them to customers or to the general public as part of special promotions. To encourage businesses to use the tickets in this way, promise that an announcement will be made on the public-address system thanking the businesses that purchased the blocks of tickets. Relate that the money raised will be used by the nonprofit sport organization to assist the school's athletic program.

Time: Begin soliciting sponsors 4 or 5 weeks before the start of the sport season. Each company's promotional campaign will vary, but expect them to publicize for 2 to 3 weeks prior to the date of the sponsored game.

Expenditures: Plan to spend $250 in seed money. Create banners and signs identifying each game's sponsor(s). The tickets sold to the businesses must be printed in a large size because they will include advertising messages from the company.

Personnel (Staff and Volunteers): A small staff (1-2) and some influential volunteers (7-10) are needed to approach those individuals who have decision-making power in various businesses or corporations. Personal and professional contacts in the business arena are invaluable in terms of opening doors to the people who have the authority to make purchases.

RISK MANAGEMENT

There are no financial risks or significant liability exposure involved in this effort. The contests will be played regardless of whether any business purchases a block of tickets. However, the athletic promoters should be aware that a large number of additional spectators might strain the parking and concession operations as well as the restroom facilities. Appropriate action must be taken to avoid problems in these areas.

There is, however, a risk of embarrassment if there is a poor attendance at the event even though free tickets were distributed. Businesses are very careful with their donations and advertising dollars. They will want to know exactly how many of the free tickets were used by those who had received them. If 1,500 discounted tickets were purchased for $2,250 and subsequently given away, yet only 35 of those tickets were used to gain entrance to the game, the corporate sponsor would not be likely to buy more tickets, even at the discounted price.

PERMITS/LICENSES

None

HINTS

Depending upon their availability, tickets to any specific event can be steeply discounted or sold at face value. In those instances where the athletic administrators anticipate being left with a lot of unsold tickets by the date of the game, they would come out ahead if they sold 1,000 to 2,000 tickets to a business at a discount of 50 percent or more. If the ticket price is normally $3 per person, discounting 1,500 tickets by 50 percent would bring $2,250 more in profit than would have been realized had the tickets not been sold at all. Consider, too, that additional spectators will provide an increase in concession sales and a larger cheering crowd to boost the morale of the athletes.

Rotational Advertisement Sign

POTENTIAL NET INCOME
$11,400

COMPLEXITY/DEGREE OF DIFFICULTY
Low

DESCRIPTION
A portable, backlighted advertising sign trimmed in the sponsoring organization's colors is used at all athletic or recreational events. The space can be rented to up to 30 different companies for $500 each (or whatever the market will bear) per academic year. The sign—6 feet long, 31 inches high, and 10 inches deep—rotates to display a different advertisement every 25 seconds. Such signs have been popular at professional and major college games for some time and are now being used successfully on the small college and secondary school level, as well as by recreation organizations. The signs can be rented from a variety of companies, one of which is Rotational Computerized Automation, Inc., 122 N. Genesse St., Geneva, NY, 14456.

SCHEDULING
The sign can be displayed at all home athletic contests or recreation events and at other times can be set up in the lobby of the school, athletic facility, or recreation site.

RESOURCES
Facilities: The sign can be used at any indoor or outdoor sport or recreational site where an adequate number of spectators or members of the general public will see the advertisements.

Equipment and Supplies: The sponsoring organization obtains the sign, an extension cord, and plastic sheets that contain the advertising copy for each business. Use color photographs of the sign to promote this fundraising idea to potential advertisers.

Publicity and Promotion: Approach potential advertisers on a person-to-person basis. During the sales pitch, relate the number of people who regularly attend the different athletic or recreational activities. Explain that during these events, the public-address system will be used to encourage the spectators to patronize those advertisers who support the organization. Show a color photograph of the sign so the prospect can see exactly the type of advertising medium being offered. The number of advertisers on the sign can range from 4 to 30.

Time: This fundraising project can be organized within a week. It will take another 1 to 2 weeks to have the individual advertisement signs created for the machine. Selling the 30 advertising slots for the sign can be an ongoing process. The sign can be moved from one site to another and set up with minimal effort.

Expenditures: The rent for the sign is $3,600 a year. The cost of creating each plastic advertising sheet is $100 if the ad is black-and-white; colors can be added for $25 per. The advertisers bear this cost in addition to the flat fee for the sign space.

Personnel (Staff and Volunteers): A small number of staff or volunteers (2-3) can successfully market the advertising. These people also aid the businesspersons in creating the copy for their ads. Two people can move and set up the portable sign with ease.

RISK MANAGEMENT

There is no financial risk involved in this fundraising project. The agreement with the company providing the sign is not finalized until a minimum number of advertisers have been signed up and the money collected. Liability is also minimal. All advertising copy must be double-checked for accuracy and appropriateness. Some organizations have restrictions against advertisements for cigarettes or alcoholic beverages.

PERMITS/LICENSES

None

HINTS

The organizers should strive to sell the businesspersons a package deal involving a 9- or 12-month period. Shorter periods may be agreed upon under certain circumstances. Prior to committing to the rental of the sign, the organizers should have contracts with at least enough advertisers to pay for the rental charge. Once the sign is in use, additional advertisers can be added. There should always be potential advertisers lined up to replace those that might be lost during the course of the year. It may be easier to attract new customers for the next year when they know that you have sold out the advertising slots for the current year.

Kids' Day Off

POTENTIAL NET INCOME
$11,500 annually

COMPLEXITY/DEGREE OF DIFFICULTY
Moderate

DESCRIPTION
Youngsters (ages 6-16) within a community can be signed up for a variety of physical, intellectual, and social activities inside a school gymnasium or recreation facility. The charge to parents is $5 per child.

SCHEDULING
The recreational opportunities are available each Saturday from September through April.

RESOURCES
Facilities: A large indoor facility, such as a gymnasium or field house, is ideal. If an indoor pool is available, water activities can be planned.

Equipment and Supplies: The sponsoring organization provides equipment and supplies that enable youngsters to participate in a wide variety of activities, such as chess, volleyball, and jumping rope. A cash box, receipt book, and record book are needed. A television, videocassette player, and wide range of videotapes can be used for quiet time. An audiotape player and tapes (or compact disc player and compact discs) are useful. Information and medical forms (attached to clip boards) must be available for parents to fill out. An emergency phone list is drawn up, then prominently displayed.

Publicity and Promotion: Announcements in local newspapers and advertising periodicals, together with word-of-mouth publicity and announcements over the public-address systems at athletic and recreation activities, are used to spread the word throughout the community. Publicize that this fundraising project is sponsored by a worthy, local organization, and reveal how the profit will be used. If the youngsters have fun and if the parents feel that their children are involved in wholesome activities within a safe and nurturing environment, the attendance will grow.

Time: The activities for the youngsters begin at 9 A.M. and conclude at 3 P.M. The children may arrive at the site at any time between those hours.

Expenditures: This fundraising effort can be initiated for $100 for advertising costs and for those supplies that are not donated. The activities are conducted by volunteers, and the use of the facility should be free.

Personnel (Staff and Volunteers): A large number of volunteers and staff (30-45) serve on a rotating schedule. A school nurse, athletic trainer, or student athletic trainer should be in the facility during the hours that youngsters are in attendance. Adults and college athletes direct the children in a wide range of activities. Certified lifeguards must be present if water activities are held. The number of volunteers needed on any given Saturday will depend upon the number of youngsters signed up.

RISK MANAGEMENT

There is no financial risk involved. To reduce liability, a responsible adult should be in charge of each Saturday's activities. Check the insurance policy covering the facility to ascertain that it provides adequate protection for the volunteers as well as for the sponsoring organization. Parents must complete an information form and a medical form for each child. The local ambulance or Emergency Medical Team squad should be informed about the program, in case their services are needed.

The security of the children is critical. They may not leave the facility by themselves without written permission from their parents. The volunteers must see that the children are picked up only by those persons who have permission to do so.

PERMITS/LICENSES

Check with the town clerk or department of social services to determine if a permit is needed. Some communities or states require a temporary day care permit or a camp license to conduct such an activity on a regular basis for a large number of youngsters.

HINTS

Encourage advance sign-ups so that adequate volunteers will be present each Saturday. This is an ideal fundraiser for college athletes who wish to work with youngsters while helping a worthwhile cause. If youngsters stay during the lunch hour, they bring their own food and drink, and they eat in a designated area. Those who eat at the site must wait 30 minutes before they may participate in aquatic activities, if available.

60

Backward Raffle

POTENTIAL NET INCOME

$11,600

COMPLEXITY/DEGREE OF DIFFICULTY

Moderate

DESCRIPTION

With this raffle, the holder of the first ticket drawn receives the least valuable prize. The value of each prize increases until the grand prize is awarded to the holder of the last ticket drawn. Prizes could be anything: clothing, trips, golf memberships, cash, and so forth. The number of prizes raffled depends upon the number of items and services donated by various individuals and businesses within the community. The organization's goal is to sell 2,500 tickets at $5 each. The fact that the most valuable prizes are given away at the end of the drawing ensures that a large number of ticket holders will stay until the end of the event.

SCHEDULING

The Backward Raffle can be held any weekend afternoon or evening. This event can stand alone or be piggybacked with another activity, such as a banquet or athletic contest.

RESOURCES

Facilities: The site for this raffle must have good acoustics and comfortably accommodate a large crowd. Adequate parking must be available.

Equipment and Supplies: An effective public-address system is essential. A drum is the most appropriate container for holding and mixing a large number of tickets, but some other container would suffice. Special two-part tickets are used so that one half may be retained by the purchaser and the other placed in the container. Chairs are needed, as well as tables on which to display the prizes. Cardboard and paint are needed for creating posters. Flyers must be printed. Between 100 and 175 prizes should be solicited on a donated basis.

Publicity and Promotion: Distribute numerous flyers and posters. Businesses can display posters and perhaps sell the raffle tickets. Establish many ticket outlets to greatly increase the number of tickets sold. Approach the news media to include mention of this event in their public-service announcements. Emphasize that the money raised will be used for a good cause within the community. Publicize the value of the grand prize, whether it is a free ski trip, an excursion to a popular theme park, or $1,000 in cash. Relate that participants need not be present to win. Be sure that the public understands that the distribution of prizes will be in *reverse order* of their value, with the last ticket drawn winning the grand prize.

Time: Planning for this fundraiser can take several weeks. Allow another 4 to 5 weeks to implement the activity, including publicity and promotional efforts. The duration of the raffle itself will run between 45 minutes and several hours, depending upon the number of tickets to be drawn. Allot 2-3 hours to set up the room for the raffle and an additional hour for cleanup.

Expenditures: The prizes are donated. Plan to spend $300 for advertising, promotions, and tickets. If refreshments are provided (sandwiches, salad, chips, and soft drinks), allocate another $600. The use of the site should be free.

Personnel (Staff and Volunteers): Several volunteers (20-25) and a few staff members (3-4) market the tickets and solicit a sufficient number of donated prizes. Another 5 helpers run the raffle activities. An entertaining master of ceremonies should be chosen to pull each ticket from the drum, accompanying this action with witty and appropriate remarks.

RISK MANAGEMENT

There must be no misunderstanding in terms of how the Backward Raffle works. As in any raffle, care must be taken to ensure the integrity of the drawing itself. Responsible adults must account for the monies, supervise the drawing of the tickets, and maintain accurate records of who won which prizes, including which prizes have been distributed to the winners. Prizes not claimed during the event may be picked up by the winners at the site of the sponsoring organization during the following week.

PERMITS/LICENSES

This fundraiser is a game of chance and may necessitate obtaining a permit from the local municipality or from the state. Check with the town clerk or the police department. If refreshments are served, a food license may be required.

HINTS

Advertise that this event will provide an enjoyable and exciting evening while benefiting a worthwhile cause. To set the stage for subsequent Backward Raffles, publicize the winners of the more valuable prizes. Publicly credit those who donated the prizes; this will encourage them to contribute again the following year. Tickets for the raffle can be sold right up until the drawing begins. Free refreshments can be provided or a concession stand may be operated.

Sponsorships for Parts of a Facility

POTENTIAL NET INCOME

$11,945 annually

COMPLEXITY/DEGREE OF DIFFICULTY

Moderate

DESCRIPTION

Annual sponsorships are solicited from businesses, organizations, and individuals. Each sponsorship supports—in whole or in part—an existing sport facility or recreation building. For example, one sponsor might financially support the game room in a recreation hall, while a combination of sponsors might support a gymnasium. The available sponsorships range from inexpensive to expensive. A $200 contribution might enable a donor to sponsor (for a year) a coach's office; $500, the weight room; and $1,000, the swimming pool. If the organization secures 21 sponsors, with an average donation of $600, the net income would be $11,945 annually.

During the year in which the contribution is made, a wooden plaque with an engraved metal plate acknowledging the generosity of the donor is placed in a conspicuous location in that area of the facility that is being sponsored. An identical plaque is given to the sponsor at a formal recognition ceremony planned around an athletic event or recreation activity. Periodic mention is made of each sponsor in publications of the soliciting organization.

SCHEDULING

The solicitation of sponsors will be an ongoing activity. Each sponsorship lasts for 1 year and then may be renewed.

RESOURCES

Facilities: An office or room with a telephone is necessary to conduct business, as well as to phone or write prospective sponsors.

Equipment and Supplies: The organization creates presentation booklets (out of three-ring binders) that explain the types of sponsorships available. These booklets include photos of the facilities that can be sponsored, the cost of each sponsorship, and general information about the nonprofit group. Each prospective donor is given a booklet to keep. The use of a computer and laser printer facilitates written communication. Stamps and stationery are needed. Professionally created decals are ordered to give to businesses and individuals who participate in the program. Two sets of wooden plaques with engraved metal plates are ordered for each sponsor.

Publicity and Promotion: When publicizing the sponsorship program, highlight the nonprofit nature of the soliciting entity and explain how the profits will be used for worthy purposes. Use the booklet as a marketing tool when approaching each potential contributor. Announcements of the program should be sent to the area news media. Local businesses that become sponsors can place the professionally created decals on their doors and display the wooden plaques at their places of business.

Time: This fundraising project can be planned within 2 weeks. Obtaining the necessary permissions from the sponsoring organization's central administrators might take as long as 4 weeks. The solicitation process is ongoing. Approximately 3 months prior to the expiration of a sponsorship, the promoters should approach the donor about renewing that participation.

Expenditures: Allocate $100 for publicity and promotional efforts, including stamps, stationery, and decals. The booklets can be created for less than $30. The cost of the twin plaques (approximately $25) for each sponsor will come out of the money derived from the donation.

Personnel (Staff and Volunteers): Use influential persons (5-10) within the organization to work closely with the staff (1-2) to identify potential donors and then approach these people face-to-face.

RISK MANAGEMENT

There are no financial risks or legal exposure associated with this fundraiser. Be sure the facility or portion of the facility being made available is not already identified with a previous benefactor.

PERMITS/LICENSES

No state or local permits are needed. The organizers should seek formal permission from the appropriate administrators of the organization before seeking sponsorship for your facilities or parts thereof.

HINTS

The price scale for the available sponsorships will vary from organization to organization, depending upon the financial resources within the community and the status of the group that is seeking the contributions. Thank the benefactors frequently and publicly.

62

Parachute Bingo

POTENTIAL NET INCOME

$12,430

COMPLEXITY/DEGREE OF DIFFICULTY

High

DESCRIPTION

This fundraising project involves a group of parachutists jumping (at 5-minute intervals) onto a field that previously had been marked off into 3-foot-square parcels. On a field 200 feet by 60 feet, there are 1,333 such squares. Tickets representing each square are sold on a blind basis. That is, the buyers don't know the location of their squares until after they have purchased their tickets. Each square sells for $10 each. If all squares are sold, the purchaser of the square on which the first parachutist lands wins $3,000. Additional profit is derived from a concession stand at the site.

SCHEDULING

This fundraiser should be scheduled for a Saturday or Sunday afternoon when good weather is expected. Since the parachutists cannot jump during inclement weather, arrange a rain date. If this project cannot be rescheduled due to its connection to another event, such as an athletic contest or recreation activity, numbers representing the squares may be placed in a drum or box and the winner drawn.

RESOURCES

Facilities: The organization must secure a safe landing field, with adequate nearby parking for the numerous patrons present to see the jump.

Equipment and Supplies: The local parachute club can provide the plane and equipment necessary for the jump. Signs, flyers, and tickets must be printed. Concession items and a portable public-address system are needed, as are paint and a portable paint machine to mark the field.

Publicity and Promotion: This event is promoted through person-to-person contacts and through announcements in the media. Businesses and organizations should display signs and perhaps serve as advance-ticket outlets. Public-address announcements can be made at other athletic and recreational events.

Time: This project can be planned within 2 weeks. Allow up to 3 weeks to confirm arrangements with the parachutists and with the owners of the plane and the landing field. The selling window for tickets should be kept to 4 to 5 weeks. There should be a concerted effort to sell all tickets in advance, although squares may be sold on the day of the event. Allow 5 hours to mark the field the day before the jump. The concession stand can be set up within an hour. Allow another hour for cleanup following the event.

Expenditures: The use of the plane must be gratis, and the jumpers are volunteers from the local parachutists' club. Allow $350 for publicity and promotional expenses, and $150 for beginning inventory for the concession stand. A take-off fee (if any) to cover the cost of the pilot and gasoline could run as high as $400. The paint for the field, the paint machine, and the use of the land should be obtained without cost.

Personnel (Staff and Volunteers): Many volunteers (30 to 35) and a small staff (2-3) market the tickets for the jump. One of these people can double as the announcer on the big day. There must be on-site supervisors and crowd-control personnel (7). Additional helpers (5-8) serve on a rotation basis to staff the concession stand. A cleanup crew (5) is necessary. Three judges determine the winning parachutist (the first to land) and the exact landing place of that jumper's feet on the field.

RISK MANAGEMENT

The greatest risks are associated with the parachutists. Only experienced jumpers are allowed to participate in this fundraising effort. Require the jumpers to sign a release form that absolves your organization and its membership from liability in the event of injury. There is little financial risk involved because the tickets are sold (for the most part) on an advance basis. Check the liability insurance policy for the site to be used to ensure that it covers this type of activity.

PERMITS/LICENSES

Check with the local airport or parachute club to see if any permits are necessary. A food license may be required to operate the concession stand. Check with the town clerk or health department.

HINTS

Involving a number of parachutists (with colored smoke trailing from each jumper) provides tremendous excitement and increases the odds that at least one jumper will land on the marked field. Promoters may provide more than one prize, in which case, if five parachutists jump and three land on the field, the purchasers of those parcels divide the prize money. If none of the parachutists land on the field, the winning ticket is drawn at random.

Annual Spring Barbecue

POTENTIAL NET INCOME

$14,000

COMPLEXITY/DEGREE OF DIFFICULTY

High

DESCRIPTION

Tickets for a barbecue extravaganza are sold for $35 over the cost of the meal. The goal of the sponsoring organization is to sell between 400 and 500 tickets to adults (children are charged $10 over cost). The menu includes barbecued beef or pork, salads, rolls, vegetables, chips, desserts, and a variety of soft drinks.

SCHEDULING

The barbecue is scheduled for the spring of each year.

RESOURCES

Facilities: Almost any pleasant outdoor site that is large enough to support the crowd will suffice. Sufficient parking is required.

Equipment and Supplies: The organization supplies gas or charcoal grills and other cooking paraphernalia; paper cups, plates, napkins, and tablecloths ; plastic eating utensils; and tickets. In case of inclement weather, a large tent should be available, or the group can plan to move inside a building. Tables, decorations, chairs, and large tubs of ice are needed. Signs and flyers must be created.

Publicity and Promotion: In all promotional activities, highlight that this is a fundraising activity held by a worthy, nonprofit organization and that the money gained will be put to good use within the community. Public-service announcements and paid advertising are run in the local media, including advertising periodicals. Display signs in area businesses and organizations, some of which can sell advance tickets. Place flyers on vehicles parked in area malls and shopping centers.

Time: The barbecue can be planned within 2 weeks. Allow 8 weeks to reserve the facility and promote the event. The selling window should not exceed 5 weeks. Both setup and cleanup activities will take 2 to 3 hours. The event lasts from 11 A.M. to 7 P.M.

Expenditures: Organizers should solicit all, or most of, the food, drink, cooking supplies, and other items for free or at greatly reduced cost. The use of the site should be donated to the sponsoring group. Plan to spend $500 for promotional efforts and another $500 for miscellaneous costs.

Personnel (Staff and Volunteers): A large number of volunteers (30-50) and a few staff members (3-4) are needed to secure the site, food, equipment, and supplies. They also promote the event and sell tickets. The volunteers are then divided into groups that perform additional tasks (e.g., set up the site, prepare food, take tickets).

RISK MANAGEMENT

The financial risk is greatly diminished if the sponsors obtain the food and drink on a donated basis. To keep liability exposure to a minimum, adhere strictly to all regulations governing the storage, preparation, and serving of food. Check the blanket insurance policy of the site where the barbecue is to be held to ensure that the coverage will adequately cover this type of fundraising project.

PERMITS/LICENSES

Obtain permission before distributing flyers on cars parked in area shopping centers and malls. A food permit or a license to hold the barbecue may be needed in your community. Check with the local health department or town clerk.

HINTS

If not all of the food, drink, equipment, and supplies are donated, the organization must pay for these items. The group might also have to pay a rental fee for the site. If the organization must invest a significant amount of money, there are two available options involving the profit. First, the group can increase the ticket price to maintain a net profit of $35 per. Second, the organizers can retain the price and accept a lower profit for each ticket sold. Local conditions will determine just how much the tickets can sell for. Significantly raising the ticket price will prevent some people from participating. The sponsors might prefer to have more people involved even if this results in less profit. Once this event has become a success, it easily can become bigger and better each year. Some organizers provide music, games, and recreation activities. Others piggyback an auction or raffle with the barbecue feast.

Memorial Gifts

POTENTIAL NET INCOME

$15,000

COMPLEXITY/DEGREE OF DIFFICULTY

High

DESCRIPTION

Contributions are made to the sponsoring organization in the memory of a deceased individual. Contributions are accepted in a number of financial categories (perhaps $5,000, $10,000, $15,000, and up). In response to each contribution, the deceased person's name is affixed in perpetuity to a facility or part of a facility. For example, a $1-million contribution by the family might result in an athletic building being named after the deceased (e.g., The T.J. Jones Field House). A gift of $15,000 might result in a room being named for the individual (e.g., The T.J. Jones Conference Room). Memorial donations can be accepted from individuals, businesses, and organizations. The departed individual for whom the donation is made need not have had any direct association with the sponsoring entity. The deceased might just have cared about the areas of interest represented by the group.

SCHEDULING

This program may be initiated at any time. The effort is continuous once it has been announced to the public.

RESOURCES

Facilities: An office is needed in which to hold meetings, prepare correspondence, and make telephone calls.

Equipment and Supplies: General office supplies (e.g., stationery, stamps) and equipment (e.g., phone, desk, computer) are used to plan, promote, and implement the Memorial Gifts Program. Quality plaques to be permanently attached to the building or part of the facility must be obtained.

Publicity and Promotion: A formal announcement of the Memorial Gifts Program is made to the public through the news media and through verbal and written communication with the organization's members and constituencies. A formal document is created to describe the purpose(s) of the program and how it works. This information includes the various categories of contributions and the corresponding methods of remembering the deceased.

Time: Planning and implementing this program can take 2 to 3 weeks. Once enacted, the Memorial Gifts Program becomes an ongoing effort, with periodic updates related to its members, its constituencies, and the public. These communications serve to promote this fundraising concept.

Expenditures: The cost of creating and printing the promotional documents will be about $250. Beautiful memorial plaques must be obtained. Image is important, so don't skimp in this area. The cost of individual plaques can range from $150 to $300, depending upon the amount of the donation.

Personnel (Staff and Volunteers): Sophisticated and sensitive volunteers (2-4) and staff (1-2) are needed to contact family members and others associated with the deceased. These volunteers should be influential members of the community.

RISK MANAGEMENT

There is no financial or liability exposure associated with this fundraiser. However, contact between the sponsoring organization and the family of the deceased can become a delicate situation. When the time is right, person-to-person contact with family members must be made in a professional and sensitive fashion.

PERMITS/LICENSES

None

HINTS

Months or even years may pass before a contribution is made to this fundraiser. Nevertheless, without the formalized structure of the Memorial Gifts Program, potential donors will have no idea that such an arrangement is even possible. Staff members should not be caught without a plan should someone approach the organization with the intent of making a donation in the memory of a deceased relative or friend.

65

Toy Fair

POTENTIAL NET INCOME

$15,800

COMPLEXITY/DEGREE OF DIFFICULTY

High

DESCRIPTION

A fair is held at an indoor facility where vendors display antique and modern toys in individual stalls. The vendors pay the sponsoring organization $50 rent for this 2-day fundraiser. Additional profit is derived from the sale of concession items and by charging an admission fee of $4 for adults and $1 for each child accompanied by an adult. With 100 vendors and 5,000 people in paid attendance, the gross income would total around $16,000, plus concession income. Anticipate a minimum of $3,000 profit from the concession stand.

SCHEDULING

The Toy Fair can be scheduled for any weekend. An ideal time is in the fall, when people start thinking about Christmas. Hours are typically from 8 A.M. to 8 P.M. on Saturday and from 10 A.M. to 5 P.M. on Sunday.

RESOURCES

Facilities: A large, clean, indoor space is needed. Location is critical. Some organizers rent a municipal auditorium or part of a city convention center. Others use their own sport or recreation facility. Adequate and safe parking is a must.

Equipment and Supplies: Tables, tickets, cash boxes, record books, posters, and concession equipment, supplies, and inventory are needed. A public-address system should be available.

Publicity and Promotion: Publicity is the key to the success of the Toy Fair. Paid advertisements in the print, radio, and TV media are necessary. Area businesses can display posters and perhaps serve as advance-sale ticket sites.

Time: Planning for this event can take 3 weeks. Allow 4 months to secure a sufficient number of vendors. Expect to reserve the facility 6 months in advance. Vendors are allowed to set up their displays on Friday evening. The merchandise can be taken down within 2 hours on Sunday evening.

Expenditures: Allot $500 to solicit vendors to participate in the Toy Fair. No other monies are expended until a sizeable number of vendors have paid the $50 space rental fee. At that point, the sponsors can kick off the publicity and ticket sales. Allow $1,000 for advertising, promotions, and publicity. The concession inventory will cost $1,500, to be paid out of the money received from the vendors. Off-duty police officers (serving as security guards) will charge around $200. Rent for the facility can come to $3,000, but try to secure the site gratis or at a greatly reduced price. If the sponsoring entity can use its own facility, this major expense can be saved.

Personnel (Staff and Volunteers): Volunteers (25) and staff (2-4) are needed to secure a sufficient number of vendors, assist in promoting the event, and help to set up the facility. Five to 7 adult volunteers serve as ticket takers and troubleshooters. An additional 5 to 15 helpers assist with the concession stand. At least one off-duty police officer should be hired to provide security (in uniform, if allowed) throughout the event.

RISK MANAGEMENT

The greatest risk is the failure of the sponsoring group to secure a sufficiently large number of vendors to attract sizeable crowds. Thus, it is important that volunteers and staff secure reservations from more than 100 vendors. The sponsors should arrange to delay payment for the facility until a sufficient number of vendors have been booked and their monies received. Ascertain that the owners of the facility have adequate insurance to cover such an activity, including liability exposure by volunteers and staff from the sponsoring organization.

PERMITS/LICENSES

Check with the local town clerk or other municipal office to determine if any special permits are needed for the fair or the concession stand. All health department rules must be strictly adhered to in terms of food storage, preparation, and distribution.

HINTS

Potential vendors are collectors, hobbyists, and store owners who specialize in buying and selling toys. There are several national and state organizations and publications that cater to toy collectors. Assure prospects that sufficient advertising and promotional efforts will be undertaken. Once the fair is deemed a success by the organizers, vendors, and patrons, subsequent Toy Fairs will be easier to plan and implement and will be more profitable.

Celebrity Roast

POTENTIAL NET INCOME

$16,000

COMPLEXITY/DEGREE OF DIFFICULTY

High

DESCRIPTION

A local or national sports celebrity (coach, administrator, or athlete) is roasted by local notables and other celebrities at a formal dinner. (A roast is a friendly embarrassment wherein friends and acquaintances of the "roasted" celebrity take turns sharing jokes and humbling stories about that person.) There can be either a cash or free bar preceding the meal. Advance tickets are priced at $75 (or what the market will bear) over the cost of the food, drink, and rent for the site. No tickets are available at the door. If 225 people attend, the profit (minus promotional expenses) would be in excess of $16,000.

SCHEDULING

The celebrity roast and dinner can be held on almost any Friday or Saturday evening.

RESOURCES

Facilities: Any site capable of seating 250 to 300 people for dinner would be acceptable. Although the roast may be held at the site of the sponsoring organization, the atmosphere in a restaurant or party house might be preferable. Ample and safe parking is needed.

Equipment and Supplies: If the event is held at an established dining facility, the management will provide the food, drink, and those items normally associated with a banquet and bar (e.g., tables, chairs, glasses). A large head table is required for the celebrity and those doing the roasting. The organization must provide an excellent sound system for the event. Signs, tickets, receipt books, and record books are needed.

Publicity and Promotion: Announcements by the area media are a must. Place ads in the local advertising periodicals, and mention the Celebrity Roast at other events held by the sponsoring organization. Display signs in businesses, some of which can serve as ticket outlets. To increase attendance and reduce expenses, attempt to exchange tickets for advertisements and other services and goods. Market this event to businesses and institutions by discounting ticket prices by 10 percent when a table of 10 is reserved. Always highlight the nonprofit nature of the sponsoring organization and the purpose for which the money is being raised.

Time: Planning can take as little as 2 weeks. Allow 9 months to reserve the site and get a firm commitment from the celebrities. Publicity starts 6 weeks prior to the date of the roast, and tickets go on sale 4 weeks in advance. If the dinner is held at the organization's own site, allow 4 hours to prepare the meal. The event begins with cocktails at 6:30 P.M., and dinner is served at 7:15. The roasting of the celebrity begins at 9. Allot 2 hours for cleanup activities.

Expenditures: There should be no cost to bring in the celebrity to be roasted or those persons who will take part in the roast. Expenses for printed materials, tickets, signs, decorations, and promotion will be around $750. Payment for food and drink are paid out of the gross profit. If the roast is held at a party house or restaurant, the rental of the site itself is included in the cost of the meals. If held at the site of the organization, the cost can be significantly reduced.

Personnel (Staff and Volunteers): A dedicated group of volunteers (35-50) and staff (3-6) is needed to help publicize the event and sell tickets. A smaller group (4-7) is needed to contact the celebrities and confirm that they and other guests will indeed attend; these volunteers also help with the details of the guests' participation. A colorful master of ceremonies is needed to keep the evening lively.

RISK MANAGEMENT

The greatest risk is that the celebrity to be roasted will be a no-show. The more important the person the greater the risk, given the demands made upon celebrities. Keeping this person up-to-date in terms of the effort involved might reduce the risk of a last-minute conflict of schedule. To keep financial risks at a minimum, establish a date by which the event can be cancelled without financial obligation to the party house or restaurant. The liability exposure is reduced if all regulations relating to food storage, preparation, and serving are observed.

PERMITS/LICENSES

No special food or alcohol permits are required if the event is held at a commercial dining establishment.

HINTS

Securing a popular celebrity to roast, as well as other celebrities as roasters, is the key to this fundraiser. Getting such people involved is always easier when a supporter of the organization has some personal connection with these individuals. Take advantage of such associations.

67

Annual Fall Craftfest

POTENTIAL NET INCOME
$20,000

COMPLEXITY/DEGREE OF DIFFICULTY
High

DESCRIPTION
A community-wide festival is held in which crafts, food, and drink are sold by a large number of groups while free entertainment is provided. There is no admission charge to the 3-day festival. Approximately 25 food booths are set up, and over 200 craft vendors display their wares in stalls or small tents. Each 10-foot by 10-foot space rents for $75 for the 3 days, although the organizers may choose to take a percentage of the gross sales instead. Other profit is received through the operation of the group's own souvenir and soft drink booths and through a craft raffle. Live music and special events, such as demonstrations of pumpkin carving and apple bobbing, entertain those in attendance.

SCHEDULING
The event is scheduled for the third weekend of October.

RESOURCES:
Facilities: An outdoor site capable of accommodating over 15,000 people at one time is needed. There must be room to set up portable toilet facilities. An alternative is for the event to be held at an outdoor playing field adjacent to a school or recreation building. A large parking area is needed.

Equipment and Supplies: Posters, flyers, and large tents are needed. If parking is arranged some distance from the facility, shuttles are necessary. Vendors provide their own display tables and booths or tents. A "petting zoo," featuring calves, rabbits, goats, and the like, can be set up on the site. Portable toilets are needed. Fire trucks and police cars also can be exhibited.

Publicity and Promotion: Send advance news releases to local newspapers and ask the editors to run feature stories on the festival. Advertise extensively in the area papers and advertising periodicals and on local radio and television stations. Display posters at the sites of area businesses and organizations. Place flyers on the windshields of vehicles parked at area malls and shopping centers.

Time: Allow 8 months to plan this project. The site should be reserved a year in advance. Lining up 25 food vendors and 200 craft vendors will take almost a year the first time the festival is held.

Expenditures: Budget $2,000, most of which will go for promotional efforts. The use of the site should be free due to the nonprofit nature of the sponsoring organization and the worthy purpose for which the fundraising event is being held.

Personnel (Staff and Volunteers): A large group of dedicated volunteers (50-100) and a small staff (3-5) are required to organize, implement, and staff this complicated event. These volunteers solicit vendors, coordinate parking, drive shuttles, and perform numerous other tasks. Off-duty police officers may donate their time to direct traffic. Musical groups who want the exposure will provide free entertainment.

RISK MANAGEMENT

No animals except those in the petting zoo are allowed on the premises. This rule should be included on the advertisements prior to the event, and signs to this effect must be posted at all entrances to the festival. The presence of the local ambulance service at their own booth at the site is excellent for public relations and provides for immediate assistance to those in attendance.

PERMITS/LICENSES

Each vendor is responsible for securing the necessary permits from the local municipal or county office. Obtain permission from the shopping mall managers before distributing flyers on vehicles parked in their lots.

HINTS

This fundraising project should grow larger each year in terms of both vendors and buyers. High-quality goods for sale and fun entertainment are the keys to bringing in large numbers of people. Organize this family event so that there is something for everyone. Some organizers coordinate an antique car and truck show with the festival.

Ten a Month Club

POTENTIAL NET INCOME

$21,500 annually

COMPLEXITY/DEGREE OF DIFFICULTY

Moderate

DESCRIPTION

A support group is formed and called the Ten a Month Club. The members contribute $10 monthly for a minimum of 1 year. If 200 such contributors participate, some $2,000 will be raised monthly. This fundraiser is based on the theory that handsome profits can be gained from small but regular contributions from a large number of caring people.

SCHEDULING

This fundraiser can be initiated at any time. The contributors may pay $10 monthly or a lump sum of $120. Donors may have their contributions taken out of their bank accounts each month via electronic transfer.

RESOURCES

Facilities: An office or room is needed for mass mailings, record keeping, and periodic meetings. There must be an address to where donations may be mailed.

Equipment and Supplies: Membership cards are a nice touch. Stamps and stationery are needed if monthly reminders are to be mailed.

Publicity and Promotion: Use one-on-one contacts and mass mailings to solicit public donations. Display signs and flyers at local business sites. Announcements in the news media as part of their public-service announcements will help spread the word about this unique fundraising effort.

Time: Initial planning time takes less than a week. Mailing of monthly reminders can take several hours each month, as can the tallying and depositing of income received. Contacting those people who forget or otherwise fail to mail their contributions will consume another several hours each month. Allow 10 hours each week for volunteers to work to expand the base of contributors.

Expenditures: Expect to spend around $100 for mailing costs each month, assuming a membership of 200. Allocate $100 for flyers or posters. Some groups give each contributor a baseball cap with the letters "TMC" on it. Such hats costs $6 each when bought in volume.

Volunteers (Staff and Volunteers): A small group of volunteers (4-6) organize and implement the monthly mailings to the Ten a Month Club members. Additional volunteers (5-7) collect the contributions and maintain financial records. A dedicated group (5-10) of influential people is needed to recruit new members and contact those contributors who are remiss in their monthly donations.

RISK MANAGEMENT

There are no significant risks involved because most expenses are paid after income has been received. There is no liability exposure to the sponsoring organization.

PERMITS/LICENSES

None

HINTS

This fundraiser can be ongoing year after year. Emphasize that this effort is separate from other fundraising projects sponsored by the organization. Identify a specific purpose for which the money will be used. A small newsletter to keep the Ten a Month Club members abreast of the financial progress and to provide related information would be a nice touch.

Membership Drive for the Sport Support Group

POTENTIAL NET INCOME
$25,000

COMPLEXITY/DEGREE OF DIFFICULTY
Moderate

DESCRIPTION
An annual membership plan is devised for a Sport Support Group in which individuals as well as corporations and businesses become members by contributing money, goods, or services. Members are assigned to different clubs (e.g., the Gold Club, the Coaches' Club) and receive various tangible and intangible benefits, depending on the amount of their donations. The larger the contribution, the more exclusive the club membership and the greater the value of the benefits accruing to the donor.

To kick-off the initial membership drive, a wine-and-cheese party is held prior to an athletic event. At this ceremony, influential and cooperative people from the community are strategically placed around the room, and after several coaches and sport administrators have spoken to the group in support of the sponsoring organization, these people come forward as the first to join the Sport Support Group while encouraging the others to follow their lead. Following the conclusion of this ceremony, the guests are escorted to the athletic contest, where they are admitted free and seated in a reserved section to view the game. Public-address announcements are made prior to and during the contest, relating that more members can sign up at the game or immediately following the contest. The average contribution is $130. If 200 people join the Sport Support Group, the gross profit would be $26,000.

SCHEDULING
The kick-off drive should be scheduled for a Friday or Saturday evening 90 minutes prior to an attractive sporting event.

RESOURCES

Facilities: The site of the kick-off ceremony should be in close proximity to the site of the athletic contest. The party facility should accommodate 250 to 400 people.

Equipment and Supplies: Stamps, invitations, and framed certificates are needed. Wine, cheeses, crackers, and fruits are served at the kick-off ceremony. A superior sound system to accommodate the various speakers is a must. Tables are used to display championship trophies won in past years. Wall decorations include photographs of the organization's teams in action, large posters depicting their athletic achievements, and the framed certificate that each member receives. The benefits (e.g., tickets, parking passes, seat cushions) that will be given to those who purchase memberships should be displayed. Sign-up sheets and membership cards must be available to sign up Sport Support Group members. At the athletic contest, tables and chairs should be set up to enable volunteers to enroll members at the game; a large poster explaining the membership options and the various benefits should be hung alongside.

Publicity and Promotion: A mass mailing of formal invitations is made to members of the group's constituencies who might offer support. The board of directors and officers should be provided with an ample supply of these invitations to distribute personally to their contacts.

Time: Allow 4 weeks to plan the ceremony and distribute the invitations. The membership kick-off ceremony should not extend beyond 90 minutes.

Expenditures: Allocate $1,000 to initiate this fundraiser. The major expenses involve the printing and mailing of invitations and the cost of the refreshments for the kick-off ceremony.

Personnel (Staff and Volunteers): Influential people are the key to getting the community's big spenders (individuals and corporations) to attend the event. A large group of volunteers (30-35) supporting a small staff (2-3) of the sponsoring organization can effectively publicize the event and motivate those in attendance to join as members of the support group.

RISK MANAGEMENT

There is little risk in this fundraising effort other than possible embarrassment if a small number of potential supporters show up for the wine-and-cheese ceremony. Thus, the organizers and supporters must work hard to invite a large number of people to attend this event.

PERMITS/LICENSES

None

HINTS

Invite both men and women to the wine-and-cheese membership drive ceremony. Those people who are invited must be told the purpose of the gathering. They also are given information regarding the nature of the sponsoring group and the names of those who have already committed to attending the evening's activities. The levels of memberships in the support group correspond with contributions ranging from $50 to $10,000. Corporate memberships (and benefits) are individually worked out between the sport administrators and the corporate representatives. A flyer explaining the individual and corporate membership plans should be given to everyone during the kick-off ceremony and at the subsequent athletic contest.

Evening Out at Home

POTENTIAL NET INCOME
$29,750

COMPLEXITY/DEGREE OF DIFFICULTY
High

DESCRIPTION
Exquisite dinner parties are held at 20 private homes. After each dinner, the guests go to an exclusive country club or party house for dessert and an evening of dancing. Each Evening Out at Home is based on a theme, with the appropriate decorations. There are 15 to 30 guests at each dinner party, and each guest pays $75 to attend. If an average of 20 guests attend each of the 20 parties, the gross income for this fundraiser would be $30,000.

SCHEDULING
The annual dinner parties are scheduled for the spring. All of the dinner parties can be held within a 2-3 week window.

RESOURCES
Facilities: Individual homes must be available for the dinner parties. A country club or exclusive party house is reserved for the after-dinner party of dessert and dancing.

Equipment and Supplies: Invitations, envelopes, and stamps are necessary. The hosts are responsible for the decorations and meals at their homes. An excellent sound system is required at the dance site.

Publicity and Promotion: Send formal, individual invitations to selected persons. Make follow-up phone confirmations when necessary. Hosts of the individual parties can extend word-of-mouth invitations. Tell all guests that this is a fundraising effort sponsored by a nonprofit organization, and relate how the profits will be spent. Newspapers, advertising periodicals, and local publications can publicize this intriguing fundraising project by carrying a feature story on the dinners themselves or on one or more of the hosts and their homes.

Time: This fundraising project can be planned within 4 weeks. However, working out the details of who to invite to the individual parties and confirming the use of the country club will take considerably longer. Make reservations for the after-dinner site 6 to 8 months in advance. Each dinner begins around 6 P.M. with cocktails and a tour of the home where that dinner is being held. Dessert is served at the country club around 9 P.M. and dancing extends until 1 A.M.

Expenditures: There are minimal costs involved in this fundraising effort because the hosts of the dinner parties pay for the meals served in their homes. The use of the country club should be obtained free or at greatly reduced cost due to the nonprofit nature of the fundraising group. Plan to spend $100 for promotional expenses, and $150 to cover the cost of the first party at the country club (most of the needed goods and services there should be donated). If you must pay a fee to use the site, try to secure a corporate sponsor to foot the bill.

Personnel (Staff and Volunteers): A committee (5-10) is established to organize this complicated event. Twenty hosts are needed for the dinners. A group of influential volunteers (5-10) are needed to approach the upper level of the community's society to assure that sufficient patrons will be willing to take part in the evening's festivities.

RISK MANAGEMENT

The hosts of the dinner parties must be influential people in the community, individuals whose homes would serve to attract patrons willing to shell out $75 per. There are no financial risks involved in this fundraiser. The liability exposure is minimal as long as steps are taken to prevent patrons from driving if they have had too much to drink. Encourage the appointment of designated drivers or provide taxicab or limousine rides home for intoxicated guests.

PERMITS/LICENSES

None

HINTS

This effort is limited to those communities in which there are suffi-cient well-to-do supporters who are willing to pay the tab of hosting dinners for up to 30 people, and others who are able to part with $75 to be a guest. This sophisticated fundraiser does provide the partici-pants with a gourmet dinner and a fun evening of dancing. An additional reward is knowing that they are contributing to an event that will benefit a worthwhile cause.

ABOUT THE AUTHOR

William F. Stier, Jr., EdD, is the graduate coordinator of the Physical Education and Sport Department and of the athletic administration program at the State University of New York (SUNY), Brockport. He also is the director of the undergraduate sport coaching and sport management programs and is a full professor of physical education and sport.

Dr. Stier is the author of *Fundraising for Sport and Recreation* (Human Kinetics, 1994), the popular predecessor to this book, as well as other books on fundraising, marketing, promotions, and public relations. He also has written many professional journal articles and delivered national and international presentations on these topics. At SUNY Brockport, he teaches both a graduate and an undergraduate course on fundraising.

A member of the American Alliance for Health, Physical Education, Recreation and Dance and the National Association for Girls and Women in Sport, Dr. Stier serves on the editorial boards for *Athletic Management*, *Applied Research in Coaching and Athletics Annual*, *Sport Marketing Quarterly*, and *The Physical Educator*. He is listed in the *Marquis Who's Who in American Education*.

Dr. Stier earned his EdD in administration of higher education/educational administration from the University of South Dakota in 1972. He has also completed postdoctoral work in school law, administration, and supervision.